Life's a Song
Sing it!

Valerie Landenberger

Bloomin' Prairie Poetry

Helene Landenberger

AuthorHouse™
1663 Liberty Drive
Bloomington, IN 47403
www.authorhouse.com
Phone: 1-800-839-8640

First published by AuthorHouse 7/1/2011

ISBN: 978-1-4634-0061-3 (sc)

Printed in the United States of America

I wish to dedicate this book to the Memory of

My Parents
Arnold & Vera Magley
Mom 1908 ~ 1969
Dad 1906 ~ 1998

My Husband
Ruben R. Landenberger
1931 ~ 1980

And to the lives of our four great kids and their families

Kathy L. Woodcox
Lesa D. Crow
Lex D. Landenberger &
John Ruben (J.R.) Landenberger

And Best Friend, Bob Burr who's my biggest fan and encourager of my poetry pursuits 1981 ~ present
Married 1991 ~ 2001

~ All of you have made me what I am today ~

"I love you all ~ dearly"

And above all, I thank GOD for all the blessings HE has bestowed upon me throughout my lifetime.

Foreword
By: Janet Carmen

When my husband and I retired from working in Dallas, we looked for a place with some space around it. We were tired of the crowded highways and the hurried life of the city. We were looking for something simpler. While we were looking and thinking, the farm home that my Great Grandfather built in the early 1900's came up for sale. We really didn't think twice about buying the place. We moved to the farm in 2006, and immediately put our energy into restoring the house and cleaning up the farmyard. Not long after this, I met Helene Landenberger at a writers' session. Helene had known my family and when she heard that we had moved back, she wrote a heart-warming, emotional poem about the old family home that we revived. Read it in this collection of her poetry.

While working with Helene on the board of the Cheyenne County Historical Society, I discovered that she knew nearly every trail, creek and canyon in the county. Together we mapped the route for a historic loop around Cheyenne County for the Economic Development Coordinator. Readers can share her love of the trails, creeks and canyons in the words of her poetry.

Rhyming, cadenced words roll off Helene's tongue as she recites poetry that describes her colorful life as a cowgirl, wife, mother, grandmother and friend. Helene learned a few tricks from her dad, a whip handler/artist. She's been known to give "whip-cracking" performances featuring her poems about the Western Cattle Trail.

For years, I have admired Helene's plucky spirit, her ability to memorize and recite in a variety of settings. She is as comfortable in front of a large conference or talent show audience as she is in small gatherings of elderly residents in the local nursing home. Read her poetry and you will feel the heartbeat of western Kansas.

Preface

I have put all of the poetry that I have recorded, into this one volume. In the fall of 2010, through to the end of the year, I wrote the poems down, having to go back and listen to the ones that I could not find copies of. This volume is the complete contents of three cassette tapes and three compact discs, 1996 to 2009. Since they are recordings, I will list them as sections rather than Chapters.

I loved the recording process, the studio experience and the sound of the spoken word, to me makes it much more meaningful, but I realize that there are some people who would rather read them. These poems have come from my heart, mind and soul and I thank God for my voice and the abilities He gave me in rhyming my thoughts. Ron Twist aka Ronnie Lee Twist is my producer, friend and recording expert, and I looked forward to every trip I made to Wyoming. Then when he went back to Nashville, I thought I was done ~ Just had no desire to go that direction. But with the encouragement of some very close friends, I did that too ~ two times. The two poems at the end of the book are by another Author, but they fit in with my trail material, and I perform them often. They were written by a lady in 1943, when she went out to the Boot Hill Cemetery, read the tombstones, and proceeded to research and write their stories in poem form. Her name was Josephine McIntire, and her little book was entitled, simply Boot Hill.

Sections

Title	Form	Year	Page
Ridin' Western Kansas	Tape	1996	1
Heroes and Horse Tales	Tape	1998	27
Hollyhocks and Horseradish	Tape	2000	49
Legends and Lollygags	CD	2002	69
When the Whip Was the Way West	CD	2006	87
Rawhide and Roses	CD	2009	121

Introduction

I first became interested in what they were calling, Cowboy Poetry when my daughter's husband was working highline construction and they were in Torrington WY. She had seen a poster about a Poetry Contest in a window and told me about it. (1993)The first year I went and just listened, as that year it was just for locals. The next year I went it was open mike, so I read some poetry, and heard for the first time, Georgann Sheets. I enjoyed listening to the guys' poems but always had to *listen real hard* to catch the rhymes. In Georgann's poems, I could hear the rhythm and the rhyme and I thought, *I can do that ~ that's my kind of poetry.* Then the third year the MC of the show told me, "Helene, your material is good, but you ought to do a couple of things. You should put your poems to memory, and you need to record them, so that when you go somewhere, you'll have something to sell." That was Cowboy Poet, Butch Martin, so I ask him where he did his recording. He said "If you want to record country music, you go to Nashville, if you want to record cowboy poetry, you go to Ron Twist". Then I talked to Georgeann, and she told me "Yeah, he does a great job, and don't let the *long hair ,hippie kid look,* throw you, he <u>knows</u> his <u>business</u>." When I recorded this first Album, I'd talked to Ron, was going to Riverton, but the night before, I called him, said the weather forecast was for snow up there, what did he think about it. He said "Oh, come on up, it's usually snow in the mountains but just rain in the valleys, and we are in a valley". So, I take off around eight am, this is in the latter part of March, and arrive in Riverton about sundown. I settle in to a motel in town, call Ron to let him know I made it and he said "See you in the morning." Well, he calls me in the morning and thought I'd really be mad at him, there was about 4 inches of wet snow on the ground. I said "No, I'm here and it's OK." Rather than just giving directions, he came to the motel and had me follow him out to the studio. We had to stop once to get snow off the windshields. Then it snowed the whole day, as we recorded in his small garage studio. It was lined with egg cartons and had a booth for me in one corner, him behind the controls in the other . He was the kind of a person that made you feel so at ease and capable that it was really neat. Not easy, but challenging and accelerating! The microphone was so very sensitive that he said, "Don't you dare burp or you'll blow me out of here." There was a window that I could, see to the outside from the sound booth, and it snowed the whole day as we recorded, beautiful big flakes drifting to the ground there along the little wooded creek. He was radio announcer, Ron in the Morning, but his recording business was called Owl Creek Productions. Any way we finished the process around three pm and I started for home. I was in a heavy old Dodge Van and the roads were crusty-icy. Between Shoshone and Casper the roads really didn't bother me though as I was just high on life and on the fact that I had just recorded my first album. He had given me a tape of some music that he had recorded for a cowboy singer and every time I play those songs to this day, I get that same elated feeling. Then going through Casper it was an absolute *WHITE OUT* and only by the grace of God, did I make it through there! I traveled the interstate for some more miles but it was going to be getting dark, it was snowing and the road was snow packed. I was getting tired, so I decided to pull it in at Glenrock. Next day the snow got lighter as I went south, the roads were still crusty ice, but I just went slower, top speed probably 45, and got to Scottsbluff Nebraska. I started out south of there but it was a blinding ground blizzard, so I went back and stayed there, second night. The heated pool at the Super Eight, was sure a welcome place to be and I got a good nights sleep before going on home, the next day. One day up, three days home. Wow! But just so glad to have it done. Of course getting it duplicated, after designing the jacket for the tapes took some more time but I enjoyed doing all of it.

Section 1
Ridin' Western Kansas

Contents,

Side One
1. First Love
2. Ole Bill
3. Beetle Bomb
4. My Horses
5. The Barrel Racer
6. Joker w/ background music, Run for the Roses
7. Doc
8. Sourdoughs

Side Two

9. The Wild Rose w/ background music The River Runs
10. Before Rodeos
11. Bronc Ride w/ background song, The Strawberry Roan
12. Ride a Cow ?
13. Wild Feedlot Spill

First Love

Two young people met in the fifties,
Both riding horses it was pretty nifty,
Guy on a beautiful palomino stallion,
Girl on a little gray, pretty as a medallion.

She was eleven, he was eighteen, when he said,
"I'm going to marry her, you wait and see."
The girl was really wide eyed with awe,
But mostly for the horse, that's what she saw.

A few years later, she began to notice,
Some things that made her heart sing like a locust.
On that horses back was a good looking guy,
His hair was coal black, eyes blue as the sky.

After Saturday night shows and drives in the moonlight,
Her eighteenth birthday brought a diamond into sight.
Their love was the kind, 'til death they did part,
It was strong and true and straight from the heart.

Ole Bill

A proud and a beautiful stallion, Ole Bill,
As he stands up high on a Kansas hill,
He'll try anything you wanna hand him,
You can figure that out, by the way he's a standin'.

He came to this country an orphan colt,
But he's as strong as a lightning' bolt.
A streak of mean, he surely has got,
Over it he and his master have fought,

But when the chips are down the limit's the sky,
For that master, he'll do or die.
Many an offspring he has sired,
That carry on his spirit and fire.

His color and his heart are both pure gold,
That's why our love for this horse is so bold.
And though he's not gained fortune nor fame,
He's one of the best we'll always claim.

Beetle Bomb

I suppose not many of you recall,
A song called "Beetle Bomb,"
I think it was in the fifties,
When this race horse song was sung.
In the song this poor old horse was last,
I guess he mustn'ta been too fast.

The guy callin' the race, would name them all off,
Then at the very end,
He would say "Aaaaaaand-aaaaaaah ~ Beetle Bomb."
Anyway that name got hung, on my little gray horse,
But once we got 'im goin' he could really do the course,

Of the barrel race or the keg bendin',
What ever I ask of him,
He had lotsa heart and go, he'd follow my every whim.
I think he was Welch and Quarter, I couldn't say for shore,
But people tell me to this day, they remember the little gray horse.

We won a lot of ribbons and we had a lot of fun,
Until I grew too big for him,
And our days together were done.
Traded him for a big leggy Quarter Horse,
I had to go to bigger,
But so many memories in the back of my mind, that little horse still triggers.

Like one day, a goin' after the milk cows you see,
We were gallopin' along just as pretty as you please,
When he stepped in a badger hole and we went flip-flopin',
If I hadn't a caught the ropin' rein, there'da been no stopping',

Ole Beetle Bomb from runnin' away from me,
But I guess I was lucky like a little girl can be!
I tell you folks, he was one heck of a pony,
With him around, this kid was never lonely.

Another thing that was quite profound,
He'd caught the eye of a rodeo clown.
Buddy Heaton, a bull fighter and one of the best,
But for buyin' my horse, he didn't pass the test.

He said *"HEY LITTLE GIRL,*
GIVE YA ~ A HUNDRED FOR YOUR PONY"
Well, now to me, that was pure baloney ! ! !

I'd been offered *five hundred* to be blunt,
So as I rode on by, I just thought (*Which HAIR ON HIS TAIL do you want?*)

My Horses

I've owned a good horse or *two* in my day,
From a great big brown to a little ole gray.
There were sorrels and bays and even a white,
If I had 'em *all together* they'd sure be a sight.

The brown could cover the territory,
The gray sure was a dandy,
The buckskin, she had stamina,
The sorrels, they were handy.
For lots of years I've rode 'em,
At fairs and in the country.
Over the hills and down the gullies,
And once in a while, even in the money.

The Barrel Racer

Some folks may wonder how we barrel racers tick,
So here are the things, that make us click,
It's the sight of those barrels out in an arena,
And the sounds of a crowd, a hollerin' and a screamin!

We love that ole *whip* of the *wind* in our face,
And a horse beneath us that's movin' with grace.
For love nor money, would we trade that horse,
That carries us *a winnin'*, over that course.

When our name's called out over the air,
Our hearts beat fast, and we may look scared.
As soon as we see that red flag fly,
We say "*Come on pony ~ let's give it a try,*"

With a burst of speed, we start our run,
And know for sure that we've only begun,
For if we knock just one barrel over,
We know *that* puts us *out* of the clover.

As we check our speed and lay into the turn,
The ground comes up, and our eyes might burn.
As we round that barrel and head for the next,
We can feel our pony, a doin' it's best.

Just like an ole whirlwind we're around that second,
And can see that third and last barrel beckon.
We stretch for the last ~ the turn feels tight,
With an *OOOOH* from the crowd, our heads go light.

But with a quick glance back, that barrel *STILL STANDS*!
So "Come on Pony, let's really dance."
We head for home with all we've got,
And pass that finish flag like a shot.

Make way at the gate, we're commin' through,
Whoa, now pony that's all we do.
And as we loosen' the cinch for some easier breathin'.
We whisper to our horse, *"Pretty good start for the season."*

Joker

From a baby colt on a misty afternoon,
To a winner in the ring,
Joker was the kind of horse
That could make your heart sing.

For such a long time, twenty four years to be exact,
He was part of our family, and what a track?

He made in our lives, one we'll never forget,
From his winning ways to throwing a fit.

Jovak was his sire, Cactus Cookie was his mom,
We took him for a filly, but boy were we wrong.

So from Misty to Joker his name was changed,
And from then on, our lives were rearranged.

As a first year 4-H'er, Kathy showed him at halter,
Won the Showmanship Trophy without a falter.

As a three year old horse, her dad used him steer-ropin',
Then Kathy got goin' on barrels, and
he wasn't just a moupin'.

Little Britches Rodeos, were the time and place,
He *whipped 'em out with power and grace.*

A few bad runs he might of had,
But with the skip-step in his warm up, he never done bad.

Fifth in the nation was his rank in '75,
A barrel racin' fool, man alive

For several years he belonged to another,
But he was *not* a happy performer.

He loved his Kathy, best of all.
He'd *do-it* , for his favorite doll.

He lives on forever in our memory lane,
He was quite a horse, and *Joker was his name.*

Doc

Doctor Wierdo was his registered name, the bay gelding,
Lesa started riding him ~ a reputation she was building.

They worked together, young girl and young horse,
'Til they were ready for the road,
Their training was in force.

Almost ever day she'd ride him,
Building, sculpting ~ molding,
'Til one day they were champions,
Their destiny was unfolding.

In Little Britches Rodeo, she made a name,
In Pole Bending and Barrel Racing, their part of the game.

He was as sure-footed, of a horse as you'll ever find,
When out there in the arena,
There was one thing on his mind.

To do the *very best* that Lesa asked of him,
He was quick to respond to her every whim.

Five saddles, lots of trophies and belt buckles they won,
He helped her to be the "*Most Confident
Kid' under the Western Kansas sun ! ! !*

Sourdoughs

An ole sourdough biscuit, is about as 'good as it gets',
It's more like *real bread,* and the *flavor* never quits.

They'll raise right up in points and peaks,
And if you bake 'em just right, they're *mighty hard to beat.*

They get crusty and crunchy, yet soft in the middle,
They're as good as a 'Charlie Daniels' ~ tune on the fiddle ! ! !

The Wild Rose

The wild rose grows where the wild rose knows,
That it will not be disturbed,
Somewhere out of the way, so to say,
Maybe down by the river at the curve.

The cattle, they may try to eat it,
But soon they'll discover the thorns,
So they'll leave it alone, and there it'll grow,
While generations of calves are born.

The beautiful, delicate, pink color,
Rests easy on the eye.
The five distinctive single petals,
Are what you can tell it by,

Some say, "Oh they're not worth the time,
They only last a day,
Other roses are much prettier".
But I an here to say,

You take a bush that's covered with tiny buds all around,
When they are in full bloom,
Not a prettier sight can be found.
It's kind of like life itself,

You've got to *appreciate* every day as it comes,
Grasp opportunities as they arise,
Before the setting on the sun.

Or life could pass you by, and you'll say with a sigh,
Why didn't I take some time,
To play with a child, talk to the old, meek and mild,
Or to Smell the sweet fragrance,
Of a tiny pink rose, in the wild !

Before Rodeos

My dad was an old time bronc buster,
He'd ride 'em high, wide and handsome.
It was hat fannin', saddle clinchin',
Whoop hollerin', and then some.

There were no chutes, no arenas, no announcer, no timer,
They'd ride two or three horses, just for a primer.

Ear'em down, snub 'em up and carefully crawl on,
Then cut 'em loose, and watch 'em spook,
and ride 'em while they're a bawlin'!
There were sun fishers, high divers,
And ones that would try to bite ya,
And if they could get ya off,
They might stomp ya just to spite ya.

He'd either ride 'em to a standstill,
Lookin' out for a windmill,
Or if he thought he'd had enough,
He'd call an outrider in, to get him off.

His bronc ridin' days are over, but never are they forgotten,
In his youth, he sure could ride 'em,
If he couldn't he just bought 'em,

Took 'em home and worked with them,
Until he got 'em broke,
Then 'turned 'em' for a profit,
I tell you that's NO JOKE ! ! !

A Bronc Ride I'll Never Forget

(In Dads words, and my rhymes)
Dad's favorite song,
The Strawberry Roan was heard with this poem.

"The neighbor Bowers had a horse, he said I couldn't ride,
I was game to try, down in the barn he was tied.
We put a saddle on him, he'd never felt one before,
My first mistake was a *single cinch saddle, but wait a minute,* there's more.

He had a nasty habit, of buckin' riders off
So you *knew* he was gonna buck, no matter who got on!
And ~ now this ole horse, he *knew how to buck,*
Anyway this rider didn't have much luck.

We got him out in the open, and put the blindfold on,
I ~ no ~ more ~ than ~ mounted,
And everything went wrong !
He took a high dive, ~ ~ ~ ~ ~ but he came down alone,
My hat went a spinnin', from the saddle *I was blown.*

The cigarettes in my shirt pocket,
Were scattered like confetti,
The tobacco can in my back pocket,
OT DAMN, I'm a bettin',
Was smashed so flat by my hind end,
A vice couldn't of made it any flatter my friend ! ! !

The sleepin' wasn't good for lotsa nights,
I couldn't even *lay* on that one side.
When I got healed up ~ ~ ~ I bought that cayuse,
I *broke him to ride*, then I could use,

Him for about anything, I rode him a lot,
Hung rabbits on the saddle that I had shot.
But to this day, I remember that first try,
When he threw me so high, *DAMN NEAR TO THE SKY.*"

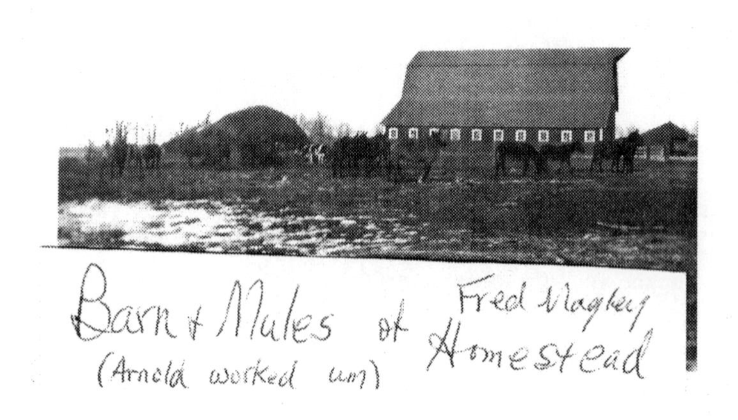

Barn + Mules of Fred Magley Homestead
(Arnold worked um)

RIDE A COW ?

My dad bought a cow, they *said he could ride her,*
So he thought one day, as he sat milking beside her.
(If she's broke to ride, just otta have some fun,)
So he saddled 'er up, when the milking was done.

Well, it went pretty good, so he took her to town,
To ride in the parade, imagine ~ riding a cow !
Laughter and surprise, were some of the reactions,
But he was happy as a lark, waving like a contraption.

For many years, they brought their humor,
To events in the area, there was always room ta,
Take Ada along and saddle her up,
Swing onto her back and maybe chase a pup.

"Arnold ~ you should have milked her before the parade,"
Was a viewers jeer as he watched from the shade.
Her udder was swinging from side to side,
The milk almost squirting people in the eyes.

Arnold pulled his hat down, and kicked her in the ribs,
"Hell ~ I didn't have time" ~ that was probably no fib.
Near Russell Springs Kansas, they were on a trail ride,
When a guy in astonishment, rode up beside,

Kind of scratchin' his head as he rode along,
He said, "Hey buddy, aint chu got that wrong ?
You see ~ Dad was leading a burrow, while riding the cow,
To which Arnold Magley just took *A BIG BOW.*

Dad's motto was "No Fools-No Fun" and he never minded playing the fool as it always brought those around him a certain amount of joy. People loved to *egg him on*. I ran across this among some famous quotes. My dad had very little book learnin' but was the kind of a guy, that when people met him, they never forgot him.

"This fellow is wise enough to play the fool ;
And to do it well, craves a kind of will."
Shakespeare

Wild Feedlot Spill

The wildest spill that comes to mind,
I took at the Tri-State feedlot, back in '79,

Mike Callicrate was the manager so,
You know we were havin' fun.
Handlin' wild South-Texas cattle,
Before the pens were done.

My husband was 'Head Cowboy',
But that day he had to be 'off',
So, at the camper he was hangin' out,
He really didn't like to loaf.

With him not riding, put me in charge,
And you take a hundred runnin' steers,
The job was lookin' large.

There was an open alleyway, I blocked that off alright,
But when they started up the west side,
They were lookin' pretty bright ~

'Bout that time it dawned on me,
(*there's no gate on the north*),
So I gave the bay mare her head,
And we went for all we were worth !

We gained on them real good,
But they were at a fever pitch,
When ole Jan, watching the cattle,
Stuck both front feet ~ ~ ~ in a newly dug ditch.

Well folks ~ the rest I tell you, was like a slow motion cam,
My thoughts were actually *this is it* ~
I'm dead ~ I know I am !

Brian Fenner, a feedlot cowboy,
Said it looked like a Wild West Movie,
You know, where they go over a cliff,
And that is not to groovy !

My face slid into the weeds,
I felt her weight go over me,
And then *I couldn't see.*

Next thing I knew, I was flat on my back,
Around me, was my rope, just slack.
Staring into the clear blue sky,
Thinking (*WOW ~ I'M STILL ALIVE !*)

Fenner rode up and said "Helene ~ lay perfectly still."
At that point in time,
I didn't argue, his advice kinda fit the bill.

He thought my back was broken,
But the word was never spoken.
He went to get help, and was gone for quite a while,
So, I decided to see if there was anything left of me,
Except my smile.

My arms and legs, *seemed* to be intact,
And what was hurting, wasn't in my back.
Lex rode up on Cockelburr, saying "Momma ~ you OK?"
I said,"I think so Lex." he said,
"I'm a getting' Daddy anyway!"

I slowly got up, my mare was on her feet,
I gathered up my rope, ole Jan began to eat.
I thought, (I'm sure glad my horse didn't end up a mess),
Then I kind of recalled, three steers *got by*,
We had stopped the rest.

The funniest part of the whole darn deal,
Mike, he thought that I was a dyin',
He said "Helene ~ she was fadin' fast."
I could scare him without even tryin'.

'Cause, you-see that old cracked rib,
Would 'catch-me' and I would gasp,
And the boss, almost thought,
I could be breathin' my last !

His words were "Get her to the hospital fast,
And don't you waste any time."
But I could tell by then, that except for my ribs,
I probably would be fine.

On the way to town, I reasoned,
A chiropractor is what I need,
So my husband took me to Pat Stuart,
That's where I wanted to be.

Now Pat, got a real good belly laugh,
As my story did unfold,
I didn't see what was so funny,
As he adjusted with various holds.

I had to sleep *real careful*,
For nights that *didn't go fast*,
But, I thank the Good Lord above me,
THAT *RIDE could have been* MY *LAST !*

Before I went to Wyoming to record my second album, Dad had been in the Good Samaritan Village for a matter of months. He always enjoyed listening to my poetry, many times with tears streaming down his cheeks. I'd say, "Do you want me to quit?" He'd say "No I like 'em."

I always dress the part of the Cowgirl Poet that I am, and when I would arrive at the Village, he would head back to his room to get his Stetson. I guess he just didn't feel right listening to all that horse and cattle stuff, most of it about him, without his hat on. The afternoon before I was to go on my trip, we visited about it and he was looking forward to hearing a new tape, when I got back. The Flowering Crab tree there south of the south entrance of the Nursing Home, was in full bloom, in fact it was beginning to loose the blossoms. The wind was blowing them away as they let loose from the tree and we observed that they'd probably all be gone by the time I returned to Kansas.

Well they were and that was the last time I saw him alive, he died the next day, of a sudden heart attack, just as he was ready to go in to breakfast. My daughter Kathy knew my producers name and was able to locate us. My husband Bob, was with me this trip, I had told him if he wouldn't complain about time and miles, he could go with me. It was an enjoyable trip to Riverton, and we were at the motel when we got the news. Bob had figured we would just head straight back to Kansas, but I said, I knew Dad would want me to go ahead and do this, so that's what we were going to do. With a sense of deep sadness in my heart but determination to complete a project, in my mind, we recorded this time in

Ron's basement as he no longer had the little studio. There was a dripping faucet in the room, he had to silence it with a cloth and Bob's sniffling about Dad, when the poetry was there, also had to be stopped because of the microphones being so sensitive. The only place my voice may have faltered a little bit, is the line, in room 107 is where I'll be found, as that was where he was found, but not for a welcome visit. We got the recording done, middle of the afternoon, and headed for home. That night we got as far as Laramie and I was on the telephone asking Roger Stone to come from Karval Colorado, to sing for Dad's Celebration of Life service as he had told me one time when I was playing some Michael Martin Murphy songs for him, that's the kind of music I want for my funeral. He was almost 93, and had been saying for years, that there is such a thing as living too long, and another saying of his was, "Don't ever get old," so in a way I was relieved for him and even though he was in a wheel chair, due to a mild case of Parkinson's disease, at least he didn't have to lay and suffer for a long time, like some people do, and his mind and wit was sharp to the end. We were very thankful for that.

Anyway with my home folks having taken care of the preliminaries ~ when I got home I started working on the casket piece. I gathered Soak Weed as Dad called them (Yucca or Soap Weed) and sagebrush then at Gerri McCurry's shop, put it together, with a miniature windmill, his old grey hat, with a rattlesnake band, one he had killed and I fashioned it for him. The scarf that he had worn at the Bird City Diamond Jubilee, when he did trick riding, vaulting from side to side hitting the ground with his feet in 1935. I also made a little sign out of balsa wood with the words "The Legend Lives On" .

So we had what we figured he would have wanted, people recalling experiences they had had with him, I played the first three poems of the new recording and did the 'Ride a Cow', and 'Final Ride." which I had just written, live. Roger Stone sang several traditional cowboy songs for us. My brother Fred MC'd there at the Bird City Legion Hall, which was full of people, and lasted from 2:00 to almost 4:00, but no one minded, and some people said, I almost feel guilty saying it but I sure enjoyed your dad's funeral. I told them that's OK, Dad would have liked that. Fred also did the reading, 'The Old Grey Stetson Hat'. Several family members besides friends and acquaintances talked of their times with him.

Cousin Bill Leach, a Friends Denomination preacher, gave the devotional, and a heartfelt tribute to his Uncle Arnold. One nephew said "Forget John Wayne, forget Jimmy Stuart, Uncle Arnold is who we loved to mimic." We had a beautiful black, horse drawn hearse, take him to his final resting place at the Bird City Cemetery. The trees along Bird Avenue were still in full color and it was a beautiful scene. No one got a picture of that so it is just a beautiful memory in our minds.

Section 2

Heroes and Horse Tales

Contents of the Cassette Tape

Side One

1. Hey Howdy
2. To Friends and Cronies
3. Village Times
4. Tracks Through Time
5. The Duke of River Valley Ranch Territory
6. Run-away-Mules
7. Cowboy Dan

Song by a Cowboy Singer Friend, Roger Stone, 'Get-a-long-Lil Doggies' another of Dad's favorites and Roger sang it and several others at Dad's Celebration of life Service in May of 1998

Side Two

Another song, sung by Roger, The Wayward Wind

8. Driftin' Sheep Weeds (Tumbleweeds)
9. Ode to the Little Bay Mare
10. Little Cowgirl
11. Runnin' Blood
12. First Trailer Ride
13. Runnin' Free
14. Oh- The Wild Rose

Hey Howdy

I'm a cowgirl poet, I hope to soon show it,
This is where our fences join,
So saddle your horse, a good seat of course,
We might just flip a coin,
To see what comes first, bring along a thirst,
For things cowboy and country and cows.
We'll jog along, almost like a song,
As much as you'll allow.
So get holt of the reins ~ feet in the stirrups dad-blamed,
Ya may have to grab for the horn !
Naw, I changed my mind,
I'm gonna be kind,
And keep you our of the thorns.
We'll ride the river, with ner'y a shiver,
We might even see some deer,
Or hit the road to a rodeo,
We'll have fun, never you fear.
So ride along and relax, and I'll make the tracks.
You sure won't have to ride drag.
I've got stories galore, and what's more,
Some are about my dad.
(Sometimes used in performances)
And I've got *one* about the flag.

To Friends and Cronies
(Dad's words, my rhymes)

"Arnold Magley's the name,
Getting' old's the game,
I've had to go to the village, a couple of falls I took,
But ~ please don't quit commin' to see me,
You know that I always look,
Forward to seein' ya come around,
In room 107 is where I'll be found."

Village Times
(Dad's words and my rhymes)

"In my younger days, there wasn't a horse I couldn't break,
But this whole dern deal, sure takes the cake,

I *go* with a set of wheels on a chair,
It's sure not like a good sorrel mare.

But I guess it's better than not goin' at all,
If I tried to walk, I sure as heck might fall.

'Round here they get me to do some stuff,
They say I can't just sit on my duff.

Like exreecizes, crafts, or sandin' wood,
Or stuffin' a toy, they say that I should,

Keep myself as active as I can,
But it's *quite the kind of job,* for a man,

Who's just been outside, most all of his life,
Makin' a livin, for a family of five.

Farmin' with horses, I sure did like,
Broke a *mule or two,* through the hard times.

Had lotsa fun, *ridin'* horses and a cow,
Feedin' some cattle and *fillin'* some haymows.

It's been a *GOOD LIFE,* but I sure don't know,
What I did to deserve this, just goes to show,

You never know the hand, life's gonna deal, do ya ?
So, make it *good while ya can, and*
GOOD LUCK TO YA !!!

Tracks Through Time

Dad tells me the 30's were rugged,
When the dust filled the Kansas air,
Sometimes it was more like night in the daytime,
And the dirt was almost more than they could bear.
There were *no crops* for cash money,
Barely enough feed to keep cows and chickens alive.
To have the food they needed,then in '38 when I was born,
He said things began to thrive.

Always makes me feel good when he says,
"After you were born things got nothen' but better".
'Course he *always was* a positive man,
Not one of your habitual fretters.

Being the farmer and stockman he was,
The '40's and '50's were good,
Lots of hard work and toil,
Brought the kinds of rewards that they should.

The '60's and'70's he continued to work,
Irrigating and feeding cattle,
Always *getting work done* by fair time,
So a horse or *a cow* he could straddle.

Along about the '80's he began to slow down,
But wait, we forgot "coon huntin" to count.
Lots of guys in the county,
Have spent nights in the woods with him,
Trailing dogs, howling the night song,
'Til the flashlights, they grew dim.

He's done a lot of whip crackin' and snake killin',
I'm talkin' the rattlesnake kind.
Some called him a living legend,
To me *he's just the BEST DAD you could find !*

The Duke of River Valley Ranch Territory

Gale Walz? I've known him most all of his life,
Kind of surprised me' when he finally took a wife.
Always on the go, knows no other way,
When he's out there workin', it really isn't safe ~
To get in *HIS* pathway, when he says, "Come-on-Hurry."
If ya get in his way, you're liable to get up seein' blurry.

At Riverside, one time, I was razzin' him in fun,
That he'd otta extend the line, maybe have a son.
Although I was kind of cringin' at *another* Gale Walz,
He said, "NO ~ no time gotta clean the stalls,"
In what seemed like not a very long while,
I heard, they *had* started a family, and Gale had a smile.

I razzed him again, "Finally take my advise" ?
"It better be a boy"; he said real wise.
Next time I saw him, he said "Emily Rose, she's so cute."
He forgot the boy stuff, he was tootin' his flute.
Well, some of you know the rest of the Wild Walz Story,
Next came a son, R.L. in his glory.

Now - our Gale Walz is quite a character,
He's kind of like a ride, on a run-away-chariot.
Five o'clock on Friday, and nothing' done,
We need five more loads, we're not out here for fun!
He'll drink some Scotch, if you get him plumb stopped,
And any story you tell, he's gonna top.

Top of the line bulls, good horses and cows,
Gale Walz is *ALMOST MORE* than the law allow.

RUN - AWAY - MULES

The spreader sat around, as old as the ground,
But once in a while it was brought.
To hitch up a team, training the theme,
Gears froze up, it was thought.

Butch was asked to help, had since he was a whelp,
His dad handled horses and mules.
Once in a while, Lyle would smile,
When Butch bit the dust, kind of built some fuel.

To kindle the flame, the excuse wasn't lame,
There came a *gleam* in his eyes.
When Lyle said "Let 'em run," Butch saw it as *fun*,
And his spirit was as high as the sky.

On a twenty foot rope, he had some hope,
Of seeing them really stretch out.
His horse was ready, Lyle held the lines steady,
It was a go, without a doubt.

To spread manure, to be sure,
Was *not* the main intent.
To break those mules, he was nobodies fool.
Many hours with them were spent.

I'm talkin' about Lyle Ewing, yeah-
He knew what he was doing,
But it got a little western *that* day.
Butch tells the story, it was not hunky dory,
When the mules decided to run away !

The spreader was chosen for weight,
But it was not the kind of freight,
That was going to stay on the bed.
The *tempo* was a risin', and it was really *quite* surprisin'
When the manure began a flying overhead ! ! !

On and on the went, they were *hell bent*,
It wasn't what you'd call fun,
Lyle was see-sawin' the lines, they were runnin' real fine,
When he said something like son-on-gun!

The time seemed to drag, in the tugs there was no lag,
The dry manure continued to go,
Those mules were full speed, the pullin' they didn't heed,
It was really quite a show.

Butch headed 'em for a ledge,

And when they cleared the edge,
The spreader was on the *fly away*.
Lyle was a swearin, and Butch was a darin',
To get his butt kicked that day.

Lyle rode it through, what else could he do?
But his patients had worn *real* thin.
When Butch go 'em stopped, Lyle came down from the top,
And said "*DON'T YOU EVER DO THAT AGAIN.*"

Cowboy Dan

Let me tell you about a cowboy, that I know,
A whale of a good hand, and it sure does show,
Ridin' those hills south of Benkelman, Nebraska,
No job's too tough, from here to Alaska.

He rides good horses, with lotsa cow sense,
Natural born to the saddle, hardly ever rests.
Dan Donahue's the name this guy carries abound,
He'll haul your cattle, bale your hay,
Or at the horse sale be found.

But this one day, ole Dan's luck 'bout ran out,
Things were a lookin' bad, there's no doubt.
They za gatherin' cattle on the Bar + Bar ranch,
Over hills, down the draws, leavin' nothing' to chance.

When a steer cut across, a small dam on the run,
Dan hot on his tail, in the mid-day sun.
WELL ~ the sand bar gave-way, 'neath his horses feet,
Into the *WATER THEY SLID, AND IT WAS DEEP ! ! !*
To hear the guys tell-it, all that remained was his hat,
A floatin' on the surface, and that was that !
Just a hat on the water, and the steer getting' away,
Durn near thought we'de lost ole Dan,
A*nd* his horse that day.

'Cause Dan don't swim,
And we was wonderin''bout his horse,
The steer had stopped and was lookin' back 'a course,
Like what's goin' on, I thought they was after me!
Now I look back, and nothin' I see.

'Til the floundering pair, came back to the top,
Then the steer ran again, like a *shot in the dark.*
They came outta the water a spittin' and a sputterin',
To think of it today, Dan Donahue's a shutterin'.

Well ~ when everything was said and done,
Guys were slappin' their legs a laughin' and a makin' fun,
Said, "Ole Donahue, he just flat disappeared,
Horse was only thing, *that saved his rear"* ! ! !

Dan leaned up against the barn, takin' in some air,
Didn't know why the guys need to stare.
He *did* look like a drowned rat,
And *knew* he was gonna have to take some crap.

He propped his foot up behind his hind end,
Water ran out his boot top, and they laughed again.
With friends like these, a guy *could* get down trodden,
But when there's cattle work to do again,
Guess who'll be proddin'?

Yeah, *OLD COWBOY DAN,* you guessed it right,
He'll stay right in there, with plenty of fight.
That was just another day in this cowboy's life,
If you don't believe me, *just ask his wife!*

Drifting Sheep Weeds

Tumbleweeds, tumbleweeds, rollin' all around,
They are the most *obnoxious* things, ever to be found !

When the wind kicks up and gets them to goin',
Here in western Kansas, it sure can get to blowin' ! ! !

I've pulled 'em out of the fences,
And gathered the wires up,
Had to *pitch* a path to the barn and almost lost my pup.

She is a Shetland Sheep Dog, and since we have no sheep,
She took to chasin' tumbleweeds, her busy life to keep.

It really was quite comical, she'd herd and chase and bite,
Then come back to me and *look*, like ~
"Did I do that right?"

Some would darn near 'roll her',
But it didn't slow *her* down,
She'd sometimes crouch and wait,
For the next one to come around.

There's a song about the tumbleweed,
Pledging it's love to the ground,
But I sure was wishin' more of them,
Lonesome and free could be found ! ! !

Ode to the Little Bay Mare

Cockelburr was a part of a special breed,
To many a kid, she was a trusted steed.

Over 30 years old and still going strong,
She had the kind of heart that made her life long.

Gymkhana, 4-H and kid's rodeo, her life,
She got out there and *went* with all her might.

Winning ribbons, trophies, buckles and saddles,
For all her kids, she'd down right skee-daddle!

All who knew her loved her to death,
And did 'til she drew her very last breath.

Little Cowgirl

We've got a little granddaughter, her name is Hailey Jo,
She's got the love of horses, right from the word go ~

She loves ole Jan and Andee, a bay and a big brown mare.
Her eyes light up like diamonds,
When you mention there's a fair.

When she see's *this* gramma a puttin' on a hat,
She *knows* we're goin' ridin' and that's a fact.

The year that she was about 18months old,
They came from California, and here is told,

She rode in the parade of the Cheyenne County Fair,
On with her gramma and don't you dare,

Think she was scared or anything like that,
She had lace-up boots, and just a baseball cap.

Don't mean to say she was just a horse lover,
She plays toys and imagines, and does she love to color?

She likes cats and dogs, and pretty rings,
This and that, and everyday things.

All spring they came from Wyoming to Kansas,
On weekend visits, it was such a bonanza !

We rode Jan in the mornings and some afternoons,
We smelled the roses and watched cartoons.

So in the parade we were ready again,
With shirts that matched and smiles that would win,

The hearts of our relatives and our friends,
Who came to watch us from the four winds.

Hailey turned three in the spring of '94,
She's a little sweetie, that we adore.

Runnin' Blood

We hauled our mares to Oklahoma,
To get the runnin' blood,
The sire was a *Joe Reed* son, Joak,
And this brought on a flood.

Of good hearted horses, with spirit that was to endure,
Lots of cow work and competition,
With satisfaction to be sure.

Kathy's Mitzie , daughter of Ole Bill,
Our Wagoner bred mare, a sorrel.
Carried the runnin' blood on down to Jovak,
Then to Joker, who was born to run barrels.

By kind of an accident and good luck ,
We got a nice bay mare,
Full sister to Joker, so Jan carried the runnin' blood to bare,

On down to J. R.'s Amaretto, Kathy calls her Andee,
Who had a filly in May of '95,
Mitzie is her name and she's a dandy.

First Trailer Ride

I'm just a baby colt you see,
Two months old and running free,
'Course, I'm with mom, and my grandma,
People say I'm 'bout as pretty a filly as they ever saw.
On kind of a cloudy and rainy day,
We were up in the corral, passin' the time away.
When in the yard of Dizzy Ranch,
She came a drivin', we didn't have a chance!

To high-tail it, to the pasture and get away,
Mom and grandma just stood there as if to say,
That gal, she's OK ~ she feeds us and stuff,
They let her shut the gate, and there we were stuck!

I thought maybe she was going to leave us alone,
She hauled that paint mare, from across the road.
She was gone for about an hour I think,
When she came back, I wondered about the stink!

That Van gives off, kind of a funny smell,
'Cordin' to mom and grandma, you'd think it was swell.
They put their ears toward her and nickered real loud.
You'd think of that trailer they were proud.

Now grandma is special to mom and me,
So when she caught and tied her, we wanted to see
Well, before I knew what was goin' on,
I was in that trailer, beside my mom!

She shut that noisy gate, *behind* us I guess.
To my way of thinking, we were in a real mess!
I guess it must be part of our lives or somethin',
'Cause up the road we went a bouncing' and a bumpin'.

We went around by town, and was there for quite a while,
They put a *halter on me,* then they *all had smiles !*
We came to this place, looked real *different* to me.
But I'm with mom and grandma, that's where I want to be.

I jumped out of that thing, and onto the ground,
Looked all around, then felt kind of proud!
I guess it OK, we're still alive,
She gave us alfalfa and grain and it tasted *Real Fine.*

Runnin' Free

Hailey's colt, we'd watched her grow from her birth,
Lot's of hopes and dreams, we had for her here on earth.
The fine runnin' blood rushed through her veins,
But everything stopped one day in May.

Mitzie was with us not quite a year,
A delightful colt, had no fear,
Would run and jump and buck and kick.
With her mom and grandma, not missin' a lick.

One time we stopped at Dizzy Ranch to check,
She came up to us, right on deck.
To get some pettin' maybe a bite of grain.
Then lick the salt block, back to the pasture again.

When Lesa came home to visit, we went out to see,
The horses one afternoon, they were as pretty as could be.
Of the parting gesture that day, we'll be fond,
We had fed and petted them, down by the pond.

The mares went off, to graze again,
The colt came back to give us a grin,
She'd come up to the Van, touch it with her nose,
Then whirl and run and we now suppose,

She was saying "Good by, I'm horse heaven bound,"
Perhaps with Joker is where she'll be found.

Not once but three times, she gave us that show,
She'd whirl and buck and run to and fro.
It's hard to understand, why it came to be.
But her *SPIRIT* is with us, though it's *RUNNING FREE.*

Oh ~ The Wild Rose

The wild rose grows down by the river,
It is *such* a soft pink color,
One of the most beautiful wildflowers,
That you could ever discover.

Oh the Wild Rose, The Wild Rose,
A most elusive treasure,
If you should chance to come across it,
It will be *your* pleasure.

This rose is a lot like life it's self,
You've got to catch the opportunity,
To see them when they are in bloom,
Among the wild flower community.

Or one day they'll be gone,
Not to bloom again 'til next year.
So go out and smell the *sweet fragrance,*
With someone you hold dear.

The drive to make this recording was even more beautiful, as I had to go on up to Dubois, in Wyoming. It is northwest of Riverton almost to Yellowstone National Park, and the sheer red rock cliffs are breathtaking. As I rounded this one curve, there stood some beautiful Big Horned Sheep. The motel where I stayed consisted of log cabins right along a fast moving stream. Ron lived outside of town to the west, and his too, was a log dwelling with those huge red rock cliffs to the west of it.

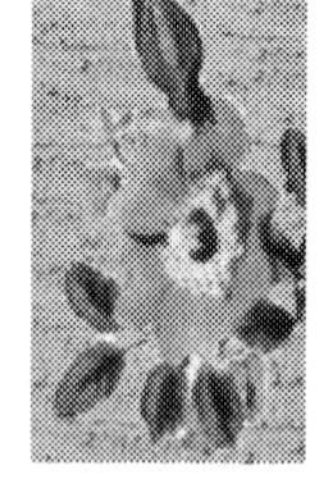

Section 3

Hollyhocks and Horseradish

Introduction (To the cassette tape)

This *(Album)* group of poems is intended to "Stir the Soul" to remember and appreciate your parents, whether still with you or gone-on to a better place. To be aware of your surroundings, many times, taken for granted, like a Sunset, a developing child, your Country, or a person you rely on like your local vet. As you *(listen to)* read Hollyhocks and Horseradish, remember to "Relish" the past, but don't forget to keep the "Kick" in the present and to appreciate another day as it dawns and presents a whole new set of challenges.

Contents

Song

To the Tune of, The Old Chisholm Trail.

My dad was a cowpuncher in his day,
A pushin' those cattle and a roundin' up strays,

Chorus

Come-a-ti-yi-Yipeee, Yipeee, Yipee, Yipee
Yae , Come-a-ti-yi-hi-Yipee, Yipee, Yae

He'd take on the job, smiling' at the land,
Blue eye's a sparklin and a whip in his hand.

Chorus

The trails were some times dusty and long,
If he had a good notion, he'd sing a song,

Chorus

He couldn't carry a tune in a bucket or a bag,
But it kept the cattle movin', they wouldn't lag.

Chorus

The old timers say, young "Arnie" was a hand,
He'd ride the ranges to beat the band.

(*Whistle* the Tune to the Chorus, to finish)

Whip Crackin'
(Dad's words and my rhymes)

When it comes to whip handlin', I had a lot of fun,
I did it a lot, sometimes at night, mostly under the sun.

A bull whip was just part of your 'driving gear',
Whether it was mules, horses or cows, never you fear,

They'll respect the sound of a whip a crackin'
And for getting' 'em on the move, you won't be lackin',

There came a time, I think in the '50's,
When a circus man showed me some tricks real nifty.

Ta get plumb accurate with a whip, takes some practice.
Lotsa Sunday afternoons it was a fact - us -

People was a learnin' how it was done,
Then we went to the Fair, to perform just for fun.

Cutting' paper from the hands, of my son or daughter,
Or ashes off a cigarette or cap from a bottle.

Of coke held out between his legs to the back,
He'd act like it stung him, and that'd get a laugh.

A course *there are* tricks to every trade,
We had a few, we didn't parade.

I won't tell 'em now those times are all done,
But I always did say "No Fools no Fun !"

(Arnold) ~ Cookin' For the Odd Fellows

When it came my time to serve at Lodge,
The responsibility I didn't dodge.
I'll cook 'em a coon, hurt 'em, it will not.
It's darn good eatin' 'sides that I've got 'im shot.

He was high in a cottonwood, so a gun was the tool,
The dogs can't climb a tree, even if they try to.
So we carefully trimmed the fat away,
Then cooked him with vegetables
And apples, and for almost a day.

Come time for serving, I was right on deck,
Then after eating, they'd come up to check,
What kind of meat is that, *tastes real good.*
Sure I'll have some more, if you think I should.

After seconds, they'd insist they'd have to know,
What is was, they were eating, then they'd put on a show.
Some of the town guys, would about *gag,*
When he told 'em,
Others said "It was real good", they wouldn't scold him.

Then his best friend John Eggers, was on the sneak,
Said, "My old black *dog,*
He's *been gone* for a couple a weeks."
Then they *really* had to guess,
Racoon or dog, what a choice.
They never ask him to serve again by unanimous voice,

The Final Ride
April 29th 1998

There came a *bad* bronc named "Old Age,"
but Dad didn't let it throw him,
He wrangled and cussed him and spurred him real hard, and at times it *was* looking grim.
But he got him rode, made the whistle last Tuesday, (it was time to call it quits.)
So the great out rider of the Wild Blue Skies, picked him up, said "That was a doozy!"
One whale of a ride, you put on Cowboy, come with me now and just relax,
Your chores are all done, you've done a good job, you really don't have to look back.
"Cause you see, I'm not just the pick-up man, I'm the judge in this *main event,*
You scored him high, you can throw your hat, and really not care where it went,
They'll be OK, dear ones left behind, 'cause they're strong, and good, just like you.
They'll not cry long, sure they'll miss you a lot,
but they'll go on,
Remembering the good times just like you want them to.
So come on along to the Great Beyond, where the grass is *always* green,
Where the gentle waters flow, the wild roses grow, and the *horses are the best,* that *you've ever seen!*

Our Mother, 1969

Even though it was an evening in May,
When our dear mother passed away,

That night seemed cold, and dark, and long.
But with the new day, a bird was in song.

The first thing I saw, as dawn was brought,
Was Mother's beautiful For-get-me-Nots.

Standing straight and strong and tall,
Saying here I am *for-get-me-not.*

We loved you dear, but you couldn't stay.
So we'll see you again some golden day!

So very brave, life's battles you've fought,
Our Dear, Dear Mother, we'll forget-you-not.

Guiding Star, 1994

Mom, you're still my guiding star,
Even though you do it from afar.
For 25 years you've been gone my dear,
But in my heart, you are ever near.

When I'm feeling down and blue,
Your words to me as a girl come through.
In ways you really wouldn't believe,
It perks me up, and brings relief.

The flowers you called German for-get-me-nots,
Most call them, just those wild old flocks.
Some volunteered out by the shop,
And even in winter, it about *stopped* my heart,

To see them growing so very green,
For me, and all the world to see.
"Don't forget Honey, I'm here to say,
Make your day *positive,* in every way."

Vera's Hobbies

My mom was a crafter, she was full of laughter
She could make about anything !
She'd get hold of a pattern,
Looked like it came from Saturn,
And lots of joy it would bring.
To not only her, she even preferred,
To give them away to friends.
And relatives too, sometimes bidding adieu,
Seldom having to make amends.

Crocheting was a love, she even made gloves,
And collars, and doilies and such.
That was just the beginning, it was never ending,
She really loved it so much.
She made lots of stoles, even some doles,
Well, pineapple pattern anyway,
In centerpieces, to set pretty dishes,
She was a marvel, I'll say !

Tablecloth blocks, she made a lot,
Dad would sometimes tease her in fun,
I'll dig a foot a day, and I'll sure as heck say,
I'll hit oil, before you get *that* done.
But do you know what? That theory got shot.
Needless to say, he *never* struck oil !
But Mom got them done, and would lend to fun,
While dad was tilling the soil.

Quilting, another art, only the start,
Of many a beautiful bed cover.
There were sew together blocks, and applique lots,
Always new patterns to discover.
At Holiday Fairs, she always would share,
All of her new treasures,
A Santa, a sleigh, or a new *tree-way,*
The joy you could hardly measure.

Of course there was sewing, always a going,
Everyday things and mending,
But it was fancy work, that was her real quirk,
To many a happy ending.

Sundown Song

A Western Kansas Sunset, is a beautiful sight to behold,
The brilliance of the colors, in words can hardly be told.

The clouds had rolled in heavy,
There was promise of some rain.
The layers of the heavens were like a sweet refrain.

And as the sun was sinking, the colors filtered through,
To show a bright pink edging, on clouds of navy blue.

A Western Kansas Sunset, is a beautiful sight to behold,
There's light blue coral and violet,
And below a *wonderful* gold.

You really need to be there, to know the feeling you get.
It is God's own creation , a vision you'll never forget!

Gymkhana

You take a kid, and you add a horse,
A saddle and bridle are needed of course.

They get used to each other, by starting slow,
And a friendship between them surely does grow.

They decide they'd like try their hands,
At some arena events, kind of take command

Barrels and poles are some of the events,
Flags, keyholes and goats, make up the rest.

Make sure your cinch is good and tight,
Then you can go, with all your might.

With a competitive spirit, and sportsmanship abiding.
We wish you *good luck* and *safe happy riding!*

Our Flag ~ Honor It

The flag that's made up of stars and stripes,
Red , white and blue, you can bet your life.
It'll fly 'ore this land so proud and free,
It was dearly paid for, for you and for me!

Honor it!

Whether in a parade, or by a garden gate,
It flows in the breeze, from morning 'til late.
Gives a heart some ease, as it settles to a stop.
Then stands there stately, from bottom to top.

Honor it!

'Ore a golden wheat field or prairie land proud,
It makes a statement, without being loud.
Those great huge flags you see in big towns,
Are as pretty as the statue of liberty's crown!

Honor it!

When it passes your way, if you don't, it's time to start,
To take off your hat, or put your hand over your heart.
To show respect for *"OLD GLORY"* you see,
And to be thankful, we live, in the land of the free !

Honor it !

Judy Mallet Baxter, DVM

Doctor Judy is a dandy, she is real handy,
Sides that, she's a darned good vet.
Whether treating a cat, or pulling a calf,
She'll get 'er done, on that you can bet.

A dog or a horse, and a sheep of course,
All fit into her knowledge,
Or even a hog, don't know about a frog,
But you can tell she's been to college.

She's got a heart of gold, when you have to be told,
That it's time to make a choice,
To let a pet go, when a disease has a hold,
You can tell it in her voice.

She works those cattle, makes the chutes rattle,
She's always on the go,
With a wave of her hand, and a smile that is grand,
Her personality sure does show!

Judy's not *all* hard work, she has a special quirk,
Demolition cars, she drives.
And hunting pheasant, she finds real pleasant,
She leads a most interesting life.

For a while she was gone, it seemed like *too long,*
She decided to come back to Kansas.
She's got an Alabama drawl, we don't mind at all,
We're just glad to have her back in St. Francis.

Country I Love

There's some hills out north of Wheeler Kansas,
That are very dear to my heart,
'Cause at ridin' fences, and checkin' cattle,
That's where I got my start.
As a little girl I'd ride 'em, with my daddy up ahead,
Then we'd split up at the windmill,
And I'd go for the dry crick bed.

Checkin' cows and baby calves,
Makin' sure they were alright,
And that none of them got lightning' struck,
In that thunderstorm last night !
I am sure the lucky one, I got to come along !
My brothers are at home, cleanin' the quonset or a barn.

The grass ~ it's popped an inch or two,
The wet ground smells so good,
The calves are growin' by leaps and bounds,
The way we knew they would,
A hawk is screamin' high above, it's such a familiar sound.
Probably waitin' for a mouse to move,
Down here on the ground.

OH, there's another bunch of cows, now, that makes-23.
And there's my dad, a way over there,
I wonder how many he's seen?
I love these hills, they're wonderful,
Just nothing else quite like 'em!
Sure a change from the flat lands of home,
I'm GLAD we got to buy 'em !

Dad says the grass is *better* up here.
So many different kinds.
When one has kind of gone it's course,
Another the cattle will find.
It keeps the stock a goin', and a puttin' on the pounds.
And it'll be *just the same,* when *another year* rolls around

Now that's been lots of years ago,
But the story remains the same.
Now a forth generation Stockman,
Is try'n his hand at the game.
Times have been tough,
Through the years, and we're not a big outfit.
But I've *hung onto the land,* I respect it quite a bit.

Yes my son, he loves his cattle,
And horses and those sagebrush hills,
It's in his blood to be that way, and make good ~ ?
I'm a bettin' he will ! ! !

There's an unusual land formation in our part of the country, that covers thousands of acres. The Breaks, start (just over the line in Colorado), goes through Cheyenne County and extend into Rawlins County. They were formed some nine thousand years ago, and contain loess soil. There is a species of sagebrush, that is found nowhere else in the state of Kansas and certain wildflowers that are considered rare.

The Arikaree Breaks

In the extreme northwest corner of the state of Kansas,
On up north of the town of St. Francis,

Lie the Arikaree Breaks, mostly in Cheyenne County,
It's a breath taking sight, almost worth a bounty!

You're going along, on nice smooth farm ground,
When suddenly there's deep canyons,
And the road curves around

Soap weeds and scrub brush dot the landscape,
But what you really notice, is the land changing shape.

Some roadways are so-steep, all you see is blue sky!
Then another panorama comes into sight.

Wildlife abounds, the Mule Deer grow huge,
Hunting is a challenge, they can take refuge.

In the cuts and the ravines,
And they can smell on the breeze,
Which way you're coming from, then they can flee.

There are Ranchers in those Breaks,
That have mighty fine cattle,
Sometimes without groundwater, it's been a battle.

But they're a tough sort, the kind that endure,
They'll pipe that water in, just to make sure.

That their stock do well, in those mysterious hills,
It's a beautiful piece of country, that can give you a thrill!

The West Kansas Yodel
(Echoes from the Hills, melody)

Well, I've traveled far and wide, but the best countryside,
Is right here in my Cheyenne County home.
Oh yes, Kansas is the best, in this part of the west.
Where the sunshine dances on the hills.
There was the Cheyenne Indian Nation,
Later on the Stage Coach Stations,
All of this a part of our land.

Yodel ~ *(Smokey Mountain style)*

Oh the Trail Drives, they were long,
And it sure was not a song,
Driving cattle through those rugged breaks.
Then the sod-busters came,
Staking out their homestead claims,
On the quarter sections of the Kansas Plains.
It can get as hot as blazes, but somehow it never phases,
The love for our home on the range.

The yodel

Oh ~ the deer are here again, but the antelope are thin,
And the buffalo is making a return.
How we love to tend our cattle,
And there's snakes that have a rattle,
Up north of Wheeler in those rocky hills.
And the horses, they are fine, for we've kept the good bloodlines,
All this in our northwest Kansas home.

The yodel

The winter winds, they sure can blow, and the snows we get will show,
In the rangeland and the crops in the spring.
The wild roses, they are few,
And they love the morning dew,
As they grow along the river and the streams.
Oh-Yes Kansas is the best, in this part of the west,
Where the moonlight shines on the hills.

The yodel *(with an added pattern of yodeling and a high note, to finish)*

Section 4
Legends and Lollygags

Dr. Joyce Thierer, from Emporia, Kansas, who portrays the frontier character of Martha Jane Canary, better known as "Calamity Jane" ask me to write a song for her. So that's why this section starts out with a song by that name. Gary Keeler and Arnold Magley also show up in the legends part. Lollygags is Wild Rose Poetry and song including the Kinen Guys, a memorable deer hunt and a repeat of the Sundown Song, this time with a harmony part. Back to legends, there is quite a bit about a beloved old mare "Jan", who was part of the family for about 30 years and was the last of the Ruben Landenberger trained horses. Somewhat of a tribute *to* the father of my four children, is the poem "Cowboy Spirit". Unusual Pair is the Bearley's, 1963 poem, and the album ends with one more lollygag, an original Swiss yodel song about, of all things, "Prairie Hay.

Contents

Calamity Jane
(Original Song)

Calamity Jane, Calamity Jane,
She was a rider of considerable fame,
Calamity Jane, Calamity Jane,
Reporters built her up and gave her a name.

She can ride like the wind, and shoot like a man,
And trick ride and rope, and she has plenty of fans.

She'll gamble and drink, and blow about her feats,
But in a real showdown she is mighty hard to beat.

Calamity Jane, Calamity Jane,
She loves Bill Hickok is what they say.
Calamity Jane, Calamity Jane,
She had his daughter one fateful day.

She loves Wild Bill, with a love that is true,
But being together, will never, never do.
Calamity Jane, Calamity Jane,
She is a rider of considerable fame,
Calamity Jane, Calamity Jane,
She has a reputation and a famous name.

Authors note;
I found out after recording this song, that her having had a daughter by Bill Hickok is a common myth, however she is buried beside him high on a hill at Custer SD, just the two of them. As was her last request.

Bullfighter Deluxe

Jeremiah was a bullfrog, a young Gary would sing that song
He'd really *get into* it, but before too long,
He was jumpin' in a Rodeo Arena,
Clownin' and savin' bull riders.
He was now a *real* bull fighter.

Keeler was the cowboy's Cowboy, I want to tell ya,
He could keep-em out of trouble,
They thought he was swell and,
Talk about an athlete, he was nimble as a cat,
He could *hop* a bull, there's no doubt about that.

This kid,I think a horse brought him instead of a stork,
What he and Billy Dale could think of,
Just didn't have a cork!
They'd ride their ponies longer than most everybody else,
"Slug" was plumb relieved
When Gary'd put his saddle on the shelf.

He did all the gymkhana stuff, Little Britches Rodeo ta-boot,
Won ribbons, trophies and all that other sort of loot.
Like garment bags, lead ropes, buckets and boot jacks,
Whether winning or just placing, he was always making tracks.

A good natured kid with a winning smile,
He never minded going the extra mile.
Mom and Dad would back him, in whatever he did,
Don't think she *ever* got tired of following this kid.

A Pouder- Bred gray, was the horse,
Took 'im from a tenderfoot to a veteran on the course,
From flag races to team roping, they came along.
He was just real happy to be in the cowboy throng.

After High School and Colby Jr. College.
He went to Rodeo Clown school and got the knowledge,
To work those bulls, and do it with a *style.*
That made watching him do it, really worth while!

When in his mid-thirties, he was just kind of cruise'n,
Found the love of his life, in a cowgirl named Susan.
They had a neat wedding and a good thing started,
'Til a tragic road accident and the couple was parted.

The dance was then ended, that he had in *this* life,
He had lots of good times, and a loving wife.
Many a good memory Gary Keeler left behind.
A more fun-loving guy would be mighty hard to find

This practice was adopted out of necessity, while men rode the prairies with no tools except their hands and their brains. Farming practices and drought were driving the rattlesnakes in more concentrated numbers into the grasslands.

Snake Killin'

Dad's words, my rhymes

Some people don't believe it, others have seen,
Me, kill a rattlesnake by poppin' his head off,
Works real keen.

Ya got to *be real careful-not be a fool* !
It shore ain't something I learnt in school.

A rattlers' no dummy, they can be real clever,
If you're gonna do this, ya gotta be *Hell Bent for Leather.*

And catch 'um *on the run,* shore not in a coil,
Ya leave 'um alone, if that's their foil.

But if ya catch 'im *stretched out* and a runnin',
And be *real quick* ~ not just a funnin',

Grab 'im by the tail, but you *can't be slow,*
Or that wily old rattler will steal your show.

Snap him like a whip and his head will go a flyin',
Only a few guys could do this, and others weren't buyin',

This kind of tom foolery, they said was for the birds,
But my brother George taught me, so *in other words,*

I know I did it, whether you believe me or not,
In the 30's they were thick and *I killed a lot!*

Quality Time

Pete was the name of the boy, he wasn't feeling coy,
When he popped this question to his dad.
Is it true what granddad told me,
Now promise you won't scold me,
You got to *skip school*, to go fishing with *your* dad?

Yes son, your granddad didn't tell you a fib,
And really it kind of tickled his rib,
So once in a while, they *would* go fishing.
Those times just couldn't be beat,
For both it was really a treat,

And what they had together,
Beat anything they were missing.
Now Pete's got boys of his own,
And one day young Tanner was shown,
That his birthday was the day to do it.

Turkey hunting was the game, the idea was the same,
To going to school, they just said foo-it.
When 6th grade promotion came around,
Tanner thought he'd gained some ground,
So it was plumb easy to ask a favor.

Let's go fishing today, what do you say?
To go to that deal would sure be a labor.
Whoa-now kid, I'm afraid that's a bad bid,
You know your mom won't go for that.
Griff's a teach, and you came up with a peach,

That idea is dead right off the bat.
Well you won't see me crying,
But you can't blame me for trying,
It seemed to me a good idea,
And DAD you're the best,

To heck with all the rest,
Come opening day of turkey season, I'll see ya!

Foggy Deer Hunt

I went deer hunting, one day so drear,
The fog was *heavy and ever so near.*
I left the van by the west fence line,
Then following the cross fence along, was doing fine,
To a place where I thought the deer might be,
Then walking quietly, I soon did *see,*
A *buck as pretty as a picture,*
Two doe made up the rest of the mixture.

They ran to a knoll, and *stood in silhouette,*
I aimed and *fired* and I woulda bet,
That I hit him true, but *he ran* away,
I looked and looked that foggy day.
Then I heard something, was that a snort?
Sure did cut my huntin' short.
Nobody knew my whereabouts,
They wouldn't even know where to scout,

I thought (*Helene, now don't be dumb*),
You're out here alone and it's a rule of thumb,
To let someone know where you're going to be,
So if you don't come back, they can look and see.
The cover was heavy, big tumbleweeds thick,
To find *anything* would be a trick.
A wounded deer *could* be on the fight,
Best I just leave, and get out of sight.

Dang, he was a nice one though,
That rack was pretty, I hate to go.
But I 'spose I better get back to the van,

Maybe I can come back horseback and cover the land.
On the way back home I spotted a doe,
I really needed the meat, and so,
I decided to take her, I had either sex,
My permit said she was as good as the next.

I had her hide tanned in the color dark brown,
To remember the day the buck wasn't found.
But do you know what? When summer rolled around,
My neighbor had been farming, going round and 'round.
When part of a deer head an antler turned up in his sweeps,
I said, I *did* get that buck! He handed 'em to me for keeps.

So I've got a knife that's crafted real fine,
With a handle made from that antler,
The coyotes got to dine,
On the flesh of the buck that got away,
On that foggy day, when I didn't stay !
So I've got a doe skin skirt, and a knife so fine,
To remember that deer hunt, down along the fence line.

Winter Sunrise

A new fallen snow, is something to behold,
Nature lays a clean blanket and all is told,

Of creatures moving about in their travels,
Some the mysteries are then unraveled.

A cottontail in *fright,* makes some *mighty leaps,*
As daylight comes, into the shadows they creep.

THE SUNRISE IS

An icy dark blue topped with fuzzy pink,
At only a few degrees, the snow crunches under your feet.

Such a cold looking sunrise, as your breath shows steam.
To tend to the horses, they nicker for their feed,

Later in the day the pheasants come out.
To feed in the warm sun and move about.

January can be harsh in Western Kansas,
Where the moonlight glows, and the sunshine dances.

January Colt

On Valentines Day in nineteen sixty nine,
"Cactus" jumped the fence ~ to a stallion so fine.
Wheeler bound school kids, got a firsthand view,
Of what it takes to make a colt, yeah the whole darn crew.
We thought (*Oh No*) *, a foal due that time of year?*
Western Kansas winters can be severe.
We had no stables where we lived at the time,
But as luck would have it-it turned out just fine.

The eleventh of January, the day was warm and a dilly,
The mare gave birth to a little bay filly.
We named her Jan, for the time of year she came,
Had quite a few horses then, we were in that game.
The only colt we ever got to see born,
They can usually make you miss it,
In the night or early morn.
In an empty old hog house we rigged up a heat lamp.
So the colt never had to sleep where it was damp.

We got *some* cold days that winter by the way,
But right under that heat lamp, she did stay.
Baby Jan loved that heat, soaking into her coat,
Along with mother's milk, she got some good hay and oats.
Grandpa Magley had given "Cactus Cookie" to Kathy,
She had the say-so, so she gave Jan to her daddy.
He didn't have a young horse to use for cattle work,
Ruben trained her in his fashion, and she never did shirk.

A super good cow horse and easy to ride,
She'd *do* her work and take it all in stride.
For darn near 30 years, we had our good old Jan,
A good and gentle *servant* to woman, child or man.

Cowboy Spirit

Ruben was a cowboy of a special kind,
He was as good a rider, as you'll *ever* find.
There are folks that say, he could *out think* a critter,
For getting a maverick in, he sure was not a quitter!
He could wrangle and rope and take it all in stride,
And do every bit of it, with flair and pride.
He loved riding horses for this was his pleasure,
He had a *way* with horses, that could hardly be measured.
A more positive attitude, you could never find,
Even when times were tough,
There was one thing on his mind.
To keep on going and to do you're best,
And just n*ever you mind* with all the rest!
His spirit is with us, every once in a while,
When certain things happen, we can feel his winning smile.
Ruben's kids and grand kids, carry on in his fashion,
Of accept a challenge work hard and you'll get satisfaction.
He loved his kids, from the bottom of his heart.

And took their hands
right from the start.
Live life your own way, and
be good to your *fellow* man,
But don't forget to
enjoy it, it's the only
one that you have.

Good Morning Ride

To ride the range in a jeep of a plane,
May be the modern ranchers big gain.
But to get really close to nature and God,
There's *nothing'* like a horse 'tween you and that sod!

If ya happen to be ridin' 'bout the break of day,
You get the idea of the *Cowboy Way.*
The dew how it sparkles upon the sagebrush,
The meadowlark's song is crisp and fresh!

A coyote takes off, a look over his shoulder he'll dare,
Gets the attention of the buckskin mare!
She's a steppin' lively, ears forward and ready,
You strike an easy gallop, the stride is steady.

Ridin' kind of easy, enjoyin' the sights and sounds,
A mule deer takes off, with leaps and bounds.
A hawk is soaring high above,
Far from the *cue* of the turtledove.

On down the draw, following the deep cow path,
Into the south pasture, there goes a pack rat!
Nestled close to a yucca is a baby calf,
Better not spook him, or a lot of trouble you'll have!

They can run like a jack rabbit, and *never* look back,
So *just ride easy,* or you could loose track,
Of that wiry little booger and it's no fun,
Getting him back to mama under the midday sun.
Checkin' cattle and fences, everything looks OK.
It's been a *good morning ride,* thank you God for this day.

Unusual Pair, Bearleys 1963

Of the many memories I could find,
These most vividly come to mind.

A square topped car with a dog riding on top,
Meant a welcome visit from Uncle Bob's,

I guess *Little old Joker,* liked to ride,
Up where he could see all the sights!

At any parade an attraction of course,
Was a wagon pulled by a cow and a horse.

For driving this rare combination,
We were proud to say, "They're our relation."

The memories held with fondest care,
Are the *personalities* of the Bearley pair.

Uncle Bob's jovial, joking ways,
Are something we'll remember all our days.

A memory with which you'll *always* find us,
Is Aunt Mary's tender, *loving* kindness.

And now on their Golden Anniversary Day,
We say "*BEST WISHES*" , in every way!

Poetry in Motion

Riding Jan is like floating on a gentle breeze,
Her gate is smooth, she moves out with ease.

Old saddle from many a year gone by,
Feels so good, *"Look at that clear blue sky!"*

Tall grass swishing at stirrups side,
Rocking along with the rhythm of the ride.

You could search all the way from here to Europe,
But I'll take the feeling that you get in the stirrups,

Of a good horse like this, she is *poetry in motion.*
It's pleasure riding now, but don't you get the notion,

That that's all she's good for, I could tell many a story,
From escapades with cattle, to carrying Old Glory.

But for today we'll take mild weather and easy going,
Gentle breeze in our faces, and soft sunshine showing.

That for this day, we're thankful for what we've got.
And keep on going, *'Cause we've got a lot!*

Prairie Hay
Original song ending with a Swiss Yodel.

The hay is goin' down in the meadow by the crick,
With windrows nice and heavy, things are going to click,

Oh Yea, Oh Yea, we've waited many a year,
Oh Yea, Oh Yea, the day is finally here.

The bales are formin' up, in the meadow by the row,
There'll be feed for cows and horses and extra maybe so.

Prairie Hay, Prairie Hay, north of Wheeler in the draw
Prairie Hay, Prairie Hay, neatest sight you ever saw.

The smell of new mow'n hay, is so very, very sweet,
It's one that is so very,very hard to beat!

Oh Yea, Prairie Hay, thank God for this good crop,
Oh Yea, Prairie Hay, on the meadow in the draw.

A bit of Swiss Yodel followed this Poem

Section 5
When the Whip Was the Way West

This recording was made in The Nashville Area of Tennessee. I didn't care much for going down that way, yes there is some beautiful country there too, but I just feel closed in, when I can't see very far. It was fun though recording at Burns Station, a favorite country hideaway of the old recording artists. All over the walls of the studio were signatures of the greats. Every one from Johnny Cash, and Porter Wagoner, to Loretta Lynn, and Willie Nelson. My good friend, Barb (Dankenbring) Techlenburg, from Black Hawk SD, took me on this trip in her big Chrysler 300, that her husband had given her for the previous Valentines Day. She got to be in the control room with Ron and she got a bang out of doing that. The most fun of this one was getting to play the huge Baby Grand Piano,as I recorded the Arikaree Breaks song. What a tone.

Write-up in the insert of the CD

When northwest Kansas was still Kansas Territory, it was wide open spaces and literally a sea of grass. With the discovery of gold near Denver City, new modes of travel evolved. The first poem in this section talks of that very thing in the form of the Leavenworth and Pikes Peak Stagecoach Line. The Round Top A, tells of the origin of the name for the town of Bird City. Poems on various subjects from Blizzards to a Beautiful Bay Stallion, and from a Buttermilk Pie to a Battered Old Screen Door, make up the rest of the poetry. The songs in this section, show my love for Cheyenne County in the form of Arikaree Breaks and I'm and Old Cowgirl.

Contents

This song started while I was mowing roadsides, part timing for the county, Cheyenne of course. In the summer and fall of 2004. The hills themselves were the inspiration for the creation of this little song. Going to work in the mornings and seeing how the sunlight hit's the angles of the hills and just the spirit of the place, the melody and the words both just began to flow one day. I only got a line or two at first then on the days that I didn't work. I would go to the computer and figure out some more lines. My sister-in-law Marsha Magley, helped me with a line that I was having difficulties with. Her line is All natural caves and grasses that wave. I knew I wanted to include the information that there were caves in the breaks, but a rhyme wouldn't work for me. Thanks sis!

Arikaree Breaks
Original Song

Arikaree Breaks, Arikaree Breaks, the Yucca is in bloom,
The hills are aglow,
And the cuts really show,
When there's not a Horsethief Moon.

In dawn's early light, they're really a sight,
The *grandeur* is so bold.
And when there's a haze, on one of *those* days,
The beauty is untold.

For thousands of years, these hills have been here,
Where the wind and water forms,
All natural caves, and grasses that wave,
The morning sunshine warms.

And when the sun sets, your wishes *are* met,
The evening colors bloom.
From a lavender blue, to a fuschia hue,
For sorrow there's no room.

Arikaree Breaks, Arikaree Breaks,
The rarest of brush is in bloom,
The hills are aglow, and the cuts really show,
When God hangs out a full moon,
When God hangs out a full moon.

Leavenworth and Pikes Peak Express-Stage Line 1859

When the shiny new coaches, rolled across the plains,
They rocked in the sunshine, wind or heavy rain.
The Concords were crafted in the *East*, so fine.
Then hitched up to the mules and put out on the line.

A seven day trip, stations every 20 miles,
When one came into view, I bet there were smiles.
For 'there' was a drink of water, or maybe a meal,
Then, back into the Stagecoach, what a slick new deal!

They carried passengers, freight and mail,
And left their stations on time, without fail.
The going could be tough along the river sands,
And at times there were Indians, that traveled in bands.

In our own home territory, two stations were found,
Along the South Fork of the River, Denver City bound.
What became Cheyenne County, in 1873,
In the northwest region was station 19.

Then in the southwest, station 20 comes into sight,
Westward ever westward, the desolation is a fright.
A time of jubilation when the mountains come into view,
That was when Kansas Territory's,
"Denver City,"was quite new.

For just a few months, Russell and Jones ran this line,
Then the whole route was changed, with the times.
But for that era, it was a going concern,
And our Republican River was seen, at many a turn.

Benjamin Bird

Ben Bird came form Kentucky to Missouri,
Then to far western Kansas.
With the wholesale ranching business, he found a bonanza.
The Northwest Cattle Company in
1882 was a large concern,
From the Republican to the Smoky Hill was it's return.

But open range was to become a thing of the past.
Homesteaders were moving in and they were going to last.
Then Mr. Bird had to purchase,
Or otherwise acquire the land,
But he always retained the Round Top A brand.

Timber Creek area of Cheyenne County,
Became the Bird Ranch,
This formation was by design, not chance.
He acquired lots of land, on the creeks along the way,
Including Hourglass on the Hackberry,
And The DD on the Delay.

In the passage of time,
This well dressed southern gentleman,
Raised breeding stock of the finest caliber ~ "Man!"
He rode a beautiful horse,
And a custom made English saddle
He had well bred horses,
And bulls for sale to produce great cattle.

Then in 1885 ~ he was *instrumental* in establishing a town,
That was given the name Birdton,
Later *Bird City* is the name that is found.
In the blizzard of '86, he lost thousands of cattle,
And they say he decided to give up the battle.
He moved to Oklahoma when the
Cherokee Strip was opened,
But there are descendants on that land who
Kept up the hope-and,

Through the generations,
They've *honored* the Round Top A brand.
They've done the farming,
Raised the cattle and tended *the land.*
Clinton Munn and his family, carried on in his stead,
Great grandson of Benjamin Bird,
from his foot to his head.

Wheeler Store ~ Old Screen Door

I appear to be just an old screen door,
Yes, I'm that, but a whole *lot* more !
The people that have opened and shut my frame,
Would probably kind of stress your brain.

I was on the store in Wheeler Kansas.
Some five miles east of the town of St. Francis.
Northwest corner of the state is where we were located,
From early Wheeler days to 1964 is how we dated.

There's been little tiny kids and great tall men,
Medium sized women, thick and thin,
Ones in a hurry or not especially,,
Hair a flyin', others freshly,

Done to a T or maybe a Q,
A statement is made by a woman's hairdo.
You usually tell if she's been workin' cows,
There'll be no make-up on her lips or brows.

Speaking of hair-dos, she don't have one,
It's under a hat, to keep off the sun.
She'll get thick sliced lunch meat and potato chips,
To eat on the way-another sale barn trip.

The bread was *baked* and even sliced,
From the house she grabbed it, it would suffice,
And tide them over 'til supper time,
'Cause the roast is in the crock-pot, cookin' just fine.

Once in a while the kid's in that bunch,
Ride their horses down there just to have lunch.
Then they head back to the hills and on the way home.
Check their grandpa's cattle, they like being on the roam.

Well, you can see I'm weathered, kind of tired and old.
But I like to recall these stories, least I'm not out'n the cold.
The lady here at "Tasteful Treasures"
Saved *me* for posterity.
'Cause you see in this day and age,
I am somewhat of a rarity!

*Morris version

I've seen everything from braids to beautiful long curls,
Page-boys and ducktails, among the young girls.

Then there's Della Morris, good lord a livin',
When she comes foggin' in, it's a givin',
For the dust to filter through all my spaces,
She's in like a flash, and if there's new faces!

They look surprised, as she sweeps on through,
To do *whatever,* she came to do.
Then when she leaves, I get slammed again,
Good thing I'm strong, or I'd fall off my hinge!

She's got four boys and I'll *tell you what,*
Things get a little crazy on this spot.
She might have Kelly by the seat of the pants,
Or Ricky by the ear, she'd make *HIM* dance !

It kind of appeared Ronnie's just along for the ride.
And Gary was the explain-er for either side.
Sometimes I was glad to just be a door,
To handle those little guys looked like a *REAL CHORE!*

That's all I'm going to tell of that story today,
I've got *lots* more, by the way,
But as you can see by my weathered looks,
What I could tell you, would fill many books.

Buttermilk Pie

Buttermilk Pie-Buttermilk Pie?
That doesn't sound good at all.
But just stay with me for a minute or two,
And we will have a ball!

We were at a 'Rural Crisis Seminar'
When dinner time rolled around.
With an abundance of sandwiches and pie,
The choices did abound.

It wasn't too hard to pick a sandwich,
but when it came to pie,
I tell you it was a tough one,
it was just like pie in the sky !

There was this *ONE* that caught my eye,
but with a second glance,
It looked kind of like custard,
but yet it didn't, "Oh well, I'll take a chance."

The sandwich and salad must have been alright,
but my mind was on the pie.
Then with that first bite my taste buds went wild,
this flavor was *for to die.*
It was sweet, but yet it was bitey, it must have sour cream.
No- that's not it. I just can't tell, it's a mystery so it seems.

I've gotta have the recipe, so I go to the kitchen to trace,
Just *who* had brought this delicious treat,
and look her in the face.

They said they thought maybe it was Elsie Grace,
so I made a quick inquiry.
She said, "Oh yes, it's my mother's recipe,
it's just a buttermilk pie."

Well, that was a surprise. I said,
"Your kidding." she said, "No I'm not."
It's simple to make and it'll brown up real pretty on top.

It was made a lot during the depression,
because eggs we usually had.
The sugar was sometimes a little short,
but still it didn't taste bad."

Well needless to say, I've made it a lot,
and my son-in-law makes them by fours.
So when there's a holiday dinner at their house,
you can eat more and more.

Well ~ that's the story on buttermilk pie,
is your mouth a waterin' yet?
Any time I take it to a dinner,
the pan will come home empty, you bet.

Takin' 'em Home (Magley Cattle Drive, 1953)

In the fifties the Arnold Magley family,
pastured the Herefords up-north,
Then in the fall we drove 'em back home,
and I tell you, it was worth,
All the time and effort we put into it,
'cause the grass in those sagebrush hills,
Beat anything on the flatlands of home,
and sure helped to pay the bills.

Well, this one time, we arrived down at Wheeler,
about the middle of the day,
And just as the herd was crossing the highway,
a greyhound bus came along the way.
Now, it kind of rattled the cows and calves,
and some just *froze* in their tracks,
others went a little crazy,
for excitement we didn't lack!

Now Dad was riding Ole Spot,
and they both really *knew* their stuff,
So they went to work and I tell you,
they started playing rough.
To the young girl that I was, it *was* a fearsome sight.
But for my dad and his horse,
things were a *workin'* just right.

The bus load of astounded tourists,
were hangin' and a waving' *out* the windows,
As the pinto cowpony jumped onto the blacktop,
it even scared the crows.

The metal of horseshoes began to clatter and Dad?
His whip went into a swing,
In front of that bus it was crackin' and poppin',
like it was on the wing.

The cattle scattered pretty darn good,
because the sound of the whip they knew,
But one 'Old Scalawag" was a runnin' head-long,
and *that*-just wouldn't do.
'Ole Spot' , lunged and bit 'er on the tail bone,
she decided to make a turn,
Then Dad gave her a lick with the whip,
and that had to kind of burn!

As for the bus load of people,
it was a scene straight out of the "Old West,"
They whooped and cheered and hollered,
the *time they were a havin'*, was-the-best!
The bus driver looked quite perturbed,
because he had a schedule to keep,
But I bet they talked about it for miles,
anyway his horn, sure did beep.

It's a picture that remains in my mind to this day,
and I hope to put it on canvas,
The scent of the day, the feel of the air,
the movement of the cattle.
But most of all ~ that *stretched out* cowhorse
a leadin' that bus to the east.
And my dad a doin' his cowboy job,
for the memory *it is a feast.*

As for the rest of the drive, I don't recall a hitch,
I think we let them rest a while,
once we got 'em in the same ditch.
Being kind of a warm fall day,
some of their tongues began to hang out,
So-when they filed into the home corral,
ten miles later, I gave out a joyous shout !

Keeper of the Hills

Born in the hills north of Wheeler Kansas.
And remained there for his twenty three years,
The strong and handsome bay stallion,
'Keeper of the hills' and done with "*NO~FEAR.*"

A Clegg bred mare named 'Moonshine',
And a Sugar Bars Stud were his parentage,
As an '81' colt in the rocky hills,
he grew and done just fine.
Running free or jumping cuts or climbing to a ridge.

Chivas was just a year and a half old,
When his teenage master first rode him,
There was one time they went through snow and cold,
to make basketball practice,Lex's whim.

Chivas's powerful bay body would skin along
In the moonlight or under the sun.
The hills were his home and his life was a song!
An apology for hard work other horses
before him had done.

Occasionally he's been seen chasing a big buck deer,
I imagine it was purely for fun!
For exercise maybe, or just to make it clear,
that he was the boss, under that sun.

Lex and I both moved away, in the year of '91,
So it was up to Chevis to hold down the fort,
And that's exactly what he done.
A watchful vigilance was his retort.

Lex with a family and a herd of cattle,
returned in about ten years,
So it was time to turn the place back over to humans,
Three more years and he left us,
with memories we hold dear.

Heart out at the Ranch

I know I reside in town, but my thoughts
many times are found,
Out in the hills north of Wheeler.
Between Bird City and St. Francis,
in the far northwest corner of Kansas,
Are some hills were I became a dealer,
(At about the age of nine)

Not of cards with high stakes, but to get my dad to take,
me along to ride in the hills.
The cows needed to be checked,
and dad said "What the Heck",
those hills always give her a thrill.

So piano playing got neglected,
wide open spaces were projected,
And I'd help to load horses and we'd make tracks!
For fourteen miles we'd haul,
weekly, late spring to early fall,with a single axle
farm truck with stock racks.

Yeah-I know that's showing my age,
but that was an early page,
In the life of this ole cowgirl, then dad would say,
You can just drop the gate, and I could hardly wait,
to unload my pony and be on my way.

Well-that was many a year ago,
the next generation comes on and so ~
I live in town on the corner of Denison and Second.

As I watch the snow blow in from the south,
put the coffee cup to my mouth,
My thoughts are,
(the grass will be catchin' some of this I reckon.)
Then later even more snow falls and no-wind so,
I scoop the snow from the sidewalk,
and with the neighbor make small talk,
I'm really quite content to know,
That my son now works the place,
with the help of his family in every phase,
This kind of moisture will help the grass to grow.

It's been so-dry the last few years,
snow like this brings on some cheers,
Maybe there's hope that the drought will end.
We certainly give thanks to God, this will awaken the sod,
and make things brighter around the bend.

My poetry sometimes brings on a grin,
and I go to a gathering now and then,
To share with other country people my stories.
My motto is, Been there and done That- now,
so someone else can tend to the cows.
But that doesn't stop me from thinking of them,
when the snow comes in, in flurries.

Your Shot First

It was a December day, but the sun was bright,
What I wanted, was to get a deer in my sight.
But not just any deer, there was a certain buck,
And with a little effort, and a whole lot of luck,

I'd have his *hide* in my possession before another sunset,
But just how we were gonna get him was anybody's bet.
Now that's what hunting's about, the challenge
is what's fun.
And hiking over the landscape,
under a Western Kansas sun.

There'd been a lone, young buck
that I'd seen a time or two,
And sure was wanting to find him, I tell you true.
We'd been huntin' pretty hard getting' out good and early,
so this one morning, we weren't in any hurry.

Enjoying a late breakfast, on a Saturday morning,
when a neighbor stopped in without a warning.
He was excited "Helene-I saw your buck", he said.
He just went west into the pasture,
that belongs to your brother Fred!"

We finished our breakfast and gathered our gear in haste,
and figured there wasn't any time to waste.
I had my huntin' buddy let me out
in the draw north of Randalls,
'Cause on this whole situation-we wanted to get a handle

He said he'd go back north and around,
and wait for me on the west side,
'Cause he no longer could get out and walk,
he just needed to ride.
So in my old van, he went and I was covering the land.
I looked up the gullies, and down the draws,
and I thought *Man oh man!*

I suppose that smart young buck,
has given us the slip again.
But I just kept on a goin' west, I had to keep up my chin.
Then I saw the van, a-way over there,
a makin' it's way to the fence,
Next time I looked, he was *out* of the van,
doing something, like an Indian dance!

I thought, *What in the world is he so excited about,*
I can only get there so-fast!
I didn't know what all the motioning was about,
until I got there at last.
He said, "*I saw your buck, a ways back on this trail,*
he's bedded down in the dry weeds."
To get on over there, just as soon as we can,
is what we really need!

Now Bob was so darned worked up,
and 'Buck Fever' had a hold on him,
So I knew-I- had to keep real calm,
or the prospects could be dim.
He wanted me to drive so he could look,
so I began to go over it in my mind,
Telling myself to do things in order,
or success I could not find.

Put the van in park, get hold of the rifle,
open the door careful but quick.
And make sure the gun's off of safety,
before the trigger you click.
As we proceeded along the trail, he was yakking
and saying, "The little SOB is gone."
Then about that time, he sprang out of the thistles,
and *Bob got out of the van.*

He'd said on the way,
"This one is yours, I'll let you take the first shot,
But in case you miss, I'll back you up,"
his excitement was a lot!
I stopped the van and put it in park,
grabbed the gun and opened the door.
Took about three steps to some level ground,
his rifle spoke and what's more,

The deer, at about twenty yards out,
was still a makin' tracks, then I got him in my sight.
The crosshairs was at the base of his neck,
and I *squeezed the trigger just right.*
It's a picture in my mind I'll never forget,
only time I shot a deer on the run,
At about twenty five yards,
he went head over heels and landed with a thud.

When I looked over behind the van,
Bob was standin' there with shoulders in a droop.
"Got anxious and shot-missed him by a mile,
'least *you* knocked him for a loop."
He and I spent several years deer hunting,
but I think *this one* ranks in the top.
Some of the best venison I ever tasted,
I think he'd *been in someone's corn crop.*

High Noon and Zorro

Mean Roosters

There were two big roosters out at the Ranch.
One was kind of gold and the other is black.
They would *charge at you,* anytime they had a chance.
And for ego and mean, they didn't lack.
I was feeding Lex's heifers, some corn by the bucket.
Good thing my jeans were heavy,
or my legs would have been scratched.
High Noon came at me from the back, with *quite* a ruckus.
At about that time, I was a wishin'
he wouldn't of been hatched.
I turned and hit him with the bucket in hand,
He came again-feathers ruffled, spurs ready.
One more hit, then he took *ANOTHER STAND.*
After the third hit, he walked off kind of unsteady.
Those tough ole birds will *try you,*
if you aren't carrying a big stick!
It really is kind of an agitation.
To be *on guard* has to be your trick.
It seemed like it kind of stopped the aggravation.
As time went on the roosters gained some hobbles.
Then they would just stand around
the hens looking kind of puzzled.
And it did slow down the rooster troubles.
The times were fewer that they got their feathers ruffled.
Now what's left in Zorro, 'cause High Noon *is no more,*
He tried Lex one too many times
and just plumb *lost* his head.

Walk softly and carry a big stick, means a little more,
And Zorro better watch it or he'll be the *next one dead!*

Blizzard

When the fury of nature descends on these great High Plains,
we are reminded of our smallness.

When the big white wind sweeps across the plains,
Here in Northwest Kansas, it takes the reins.

It's a *runaway horse* that's fearsome and bold,
The wind blows strong and the wind blows cold.

It does as it pleases and goes on and on.
It whips and whirls and shows it brawn.

A blizzard displays-it's wild-ugly features,
It puts us in our places down to the smallest creature.

Once again we are reminded just how good we have it.
In our push-button world all we have to do is grab it.

Some of us remember

Before electricity, television, computers and cell phones,
There was just dim lamp light and I'll make no bones,

When there was a warning one was *headed* our way,
We got things ready-got inside and just enjoyed the day.

Kansas Lands

On the 29th of January in 1861,
a state was formed under the western sun,
And that would be Kansas.

The Cheyenne's inhabited this land,
along the Republican River sands,
And that's by what is now St. Francis.

The prairie out here was wide open spaces,
then there began to be new faces,
But mostly just crossing the land

There were the stage coach lines with horses so fine.
And cattle trailing in great long spans.

Later on the towns sprang up,
the homesteaders they proved up,
And the land, it began to produce.

Their crops and livestock grew,
the tough ones made it through,
Determination they didn't lose.

The land was worked with horses,
they were the driving forces,
Until tractors put them aside.

And then the dirty thirties came,
and life to them was never the same,
The homesteaders courage did abide.

Times and methods improved,
and things were on the move,
The forties and fifty's were good.

Except, of course for the war,
then patriotism did soar,
Just the way it should.

The sixties and seventy's in their glory,
feeding cattle and irrigation was the story.
The economy had quite a range.

The eighty's and ninety's more of the same,
tough to stay in the farming game,
Then the land began to change.

Conservation of soil and fuel, became the common rule,
And ground water became a concern.

Reserve program grass and no-till, really does fit the bill,
Good stewards of the land have returned.

Dizzy Ranch Cow Wreck

On a day in the fall, a few years ago,
it was time to work Lex's cows and so.
He got the whole family involved.
I almost hurt just thinking back,
for excitement that day sure didn't lack,
For this ole gramma the grandkids bawled.

They thought it was all over,
for the cow she, bailed me over,
That was Hailey's terminology.
For corrals we didn't have much,
a spook and a bluff show as such,
Dr. Judy was doing the biology.

We had 'em goin' real good, just the way they should,
When all at once things went haywire.
That cow went out of her mind, a hole she couldn't find,
And she became a flyer.

Just moments before I had made the observation,
this would certainly not be the location,
To be if one decided to jump.
But no sooner said than done,
right there in the mid-day sun,
She knocked me flat, with a hit and a bump.

The rest was kind of a blur,
what happened I couldn't be sure.
But Kathy said it was wild.
She was riding a horse, blaming herself of course,

That would be my oldest child.
In a crash of metal , hooves and weight,
a loose aluminum gate blind was just the bait,
For the cow to take her leave.
I was underneath of it all, I was unable even to crawl,
There just was no reprieve.

The stars they were a flyin',
Hailey was hesterically crying.
Then Lex and the Vet got a hold of me.
One of my legs wouldn't work,
on my face was blood and dirt,
And I could hardly see.

They got me laid down on the grass,
Dr Judy gave me tylenol real fast,
But that leg, it felt just like jello.
J. T. and Wyatt scrambled to my aid,
I thought that I was going to fade,
But they rounded up my hat for a pillow.

Things were kind of fuzzy for a while,
I couldn't even muster a smile,
But was glad no broken bones could be found.
I just felt kind of numb, in fact I felt real dumb,
What was I thinking to be helping
with cows from the ground?

On a horse was always my place,
at least you won't get hit in the face,
My mind must be slipping with age.
To be back home it felt so good,
didn't think it through the way I should,
To anxious with this brand new page.

Washcloths and blankets were brought,
I cleaned up a little and thought,
I Guess I'm lucky, just to be alive.
After a while I wanted a chair,
I was feeling kind of poor, to fair,
And with heaviness in my leg, I did arrive,

At an obvious conclusion

It's time I start making my way,
to the house and call it a day,
I'm really feeling quite worthless.
The cattle work, they got it finished,
my suffering it had not diminished,
And I thought , *I am sure a mess!*

I could hardly move around,
it brought on great big frowns,
So it was decided that I should stay.
Wyatt was helping me *BIG TIME,*
he wanted to make sure I was fine,
He'd never seen Gramma in such a bad way!

The walking was slow for a while,
I sure couldn't walk my mile,
But a few months went by and I hardly
knew I had hurt that way.

Well, they have been building more corrals,
and he said the last operation went well,
But they got to figuring it out.
When there's cattle work to be done, Mom's conveniently gone,
But would YOU look for another bout ? ? ?

Wild Roses for You

On one of those nights a few ago,
I needed more cover and so,
I remembered Mom's quilt I had tucked away,
I knew the binding was pink, that part was distinct,
But the rest of the story, I'll have to say,

Was really such a pleasant surprise,
It put some sparkle in my eyes.
The design wasn't at all what I had in mind.
Lilly pads were in my head, but there all over my bed,
You'd never guess what I did find.

I had, had a good day of writing, kind of exciting,
Wild Rose Poetry, was again flowing.
Then to finish the day, in this special way,
It was almost like *someone* knowing.

It was really a *WOW*, a here and now,
Mom was speaking to me again.
Wild Roses for you, how do you do?
I was here all the time-*where have you been?*

Dewey Ranch West Headquarters

A piece of history is gone today,
it really makes me sad to say,
Some people care not about the past,
I guess they prefer to live furious and fast.

To make way for farmland was to be it's fate,
they cared not about it's time and date.
Just thought to be an obstruction to their farming modes,
they take corn out of there by the loads.

I had some hope, *for the sake of posterity,*
that it might be saved.
But "To far off the beaten track," some of them raved.
So all that's left is memory and very little in print.
My dad could tell of the range and how far it went.

The Dewey Range once stretched for miles,
aiming for Colorado, many deeds they did file.
A vast domain, a cattle empine, now the west
headquarteers house has been leveled by fire.

Into the 1950's a huge horse barn stood,
Sheltering 50 to 60 mounts for the
Dewey Cowboy-it would.
And from the top of that house I spoke about,
If something was amiss, you might hear a shout.

Of "Mount up and lets fo see what's goin' on."
It could be at dusk or early dawn.
Those range cattle were a little on the wild side.
For homesteaders crops, they didn't pay much mind.

My Grandmother helped cook for the Dewey hands,
When she was but a young girl, she said it was grand.
To see how they entertained and extended hospitality,
They made serving in style an everyday reality.

Statesman and gentleman with their ladies,
Came from far away places, maybe even Mercedes.
To visit the largest Ranch in northwest Kansas,
It took in *lots of land,* between Colby and St. Francis.

As the homesteaders came to farm and stake their claims,
The face of the land began to change.
Free range and open spaces were not to be forever.
Civilizatiion was moving in with lots of new endeavors.

Young Chauncy Dewey, came west from Riley County,
And was running the ranch with *flair and bounty.*
Boundary troubles with the homesteaders,
went on *for years,*
Resulting in hard feelings bloodshed and tears.

But today there-are still Deweys, their roots run deep.
In what is left of their ranch their heritage to keep.
It's a place steeped in *hard work, endurance and mystery,*
It was an early day huge ranch with lots of history.

Song

To the tune of -I'm an old Cowhand

I'm and Ole Cowgirl, from the Cheyenne's world,
Where the time was lost, between heat and frost.
Where the buffalo were killed upon the prairie wide,
The Cheyenne's could no longer use their hides.

I'm and Ole Cowgirl, from the Cheyenne's world,
From their native land, they'd soon be banned.
The Cheyenne's were driven from their home on the plains,
And life to them, was never the same.

I'm an Ole Cowgirl from the Rancher's world,
Then it became ~ about anybody's game.
The trail drives were no longer there,
The bob wire came, and made the people share.

I'm and Ole Cowgirl from the Pioneers world,
My Grandad came and staked his claim.
I'm a Cowgirl who longs for the open range,
Where there's no highways and the people aren't strange.
Yipee I Oh Ki A -O Yipee I Oh Ki A

Section 6
Rawhide and Roses

Rawhide and Roses is a collection of poetry and song that include early family goings on, a poem about my father-in-laws fiddle playing, a house that stands high on a Cheyenne County hill, and two songs about wild roses. The 'Wooden Nickle Gang' poem, shows the personality diversity of a late night K-Store coffee group and 'Happy Hog Talk' is about a couple of young ones, getting into mischief as only shoats can do. The Calf Roper, poem is about our very good friend and neighbor of the late 50's and early 60's, the way he trained his horses and lived his life. The last two poems and concluding song are about frontier people in the Dodge City area and on the Western Cattle Trail, greatest and longest of them all. The song came after reading the Kraisinger's great book on the 'Western {Texas} Cattle Trail' that existed in the 1870's and 80's. This trail in it's last two form cut through our own Cheyenne County and have been marked by my historically minded brother, Fred Magley and myself, with his unique disc marker signs.

He has marked over 400 sites-everything from Country Schools to named Creeks and Canyons, early day locations such as Indian Prayer Grounds and Military Roads/Camp Grounds and anything else that we think should be noted for posterity. Thank you for your interest in my poetry and song. My wish for you is to find a lot of those beautiful *Wild Roses* that bloom in mid May to early June, and any other wildflower that God has put out there for us to just notice and enjoy.

Contents

Song-The Wild Rose

To the tune of "You are my Sunshine."

Oh-Oh-the wild rose, elusive wild rose,
You are the sweetest flower I know,

Down by the river, is where we find you,
And that's where you love to grow.

There in the sunshine, the morning sunshine,
You bloom so pretty and so proud.

The soft pink color of your petals,
Make you stand out in a crowd.

Oh-Oh-the wild rose, elusive wild rose,
You are the sweetest flower I know,

Down by the river, is where we find you,
And that's where you love to grow.

The Landenberger Bunch

In the hills where I raised my babies,
I 'spose you could say maybe,
We made a living-but barely.
Well-the times were tough, sometimes the road was rough,
But we went on-rather merrily.

Ruben-he worked for the state,
sometimes he was mighty late,
And his supper was put on hold.
He loved to get out in a storm,
he was raised where it was the norm,
And chores went on in the snow, two fold.

In those days, Mothers didn't work away,
from the home too-many days,
But I did go into the sale barn on Mondays.
Three pies I'd bake and take along,
to the sale barn café and sell for a song,
The manager of the place, would do the same

They bragged and raved, and they did crave,
My cream pies, they were delectable.
I never revealed ingredients,
they would have departed with expedients,
'Cause they were made with duck eggs
and goat's milk-despicable!

Yep,I raised my kids on goat's milk,
they wore mostly denim not silk,
And we had four rooms and a path.

From our basement house real cozy,
we would have to mosey,
Out to the toilet for that call, then there was the bath.

We had an oblong tub, within each one would scrub,
The water had to be warmed again for the last.
'Cause four kids there did abide,
with each one we did chide,
That this is the life, we're having a blast.

Now about those duck eggs,
I guess I must have been pegged,
As a sucker in some situations.
My brother was raising the fowl,
and I didn't even growl,
When he grew tired of them and brought them to me,
he was done.

Now their count was nearly sixty,
some of their looks were nifty.
'Cause he had about every imaginable breed.
The mallards were quite the lookers,
the Indian Runners were real bookers,
And all of them were rustlers for their feed.

In those hills, the coyotes got a few,
but there was nothing else to do,
But dress them out and in the meantime use the eggs.
They're bigger and fry up real nice,
sides that they're a welcome change from rice.
To keep up with those ducks,
the kids 'bout wore out their legs.

In the bushes by the windmill, they'd nest,
and it was quite a rush I'll confess,
If we happened to catch a snake trying to get a free lunch.
Either a kid or a hen would be hollering,
if the snake was into swallowing,
And there would be excitement among the whole bunch!

The baby duck handlers, were Kathy and Lesa,
grain was the way they would teach-em,
To dive into a tank to watch 'em swim.
Once in a while they'd overdo it,
then they'd have to get right to it.
Before the *hair dryer* the outlook was grim

Next came baby goats, they always felt their oats,
And gave the whole family lots of fun,
To watch them play, black white or gray,
They'd jump and twist, 'til day was done.

One time a nanny had four kids,
then died with milk fever, she *sure* did,
So the girls raised the babies by hand.
They'd jump on a little table, oh, they were quite able,
They'd wait for their bottle and take a stand.

Toads were a big attraction, they saw lots of action,
The Landenberger kids collected them by the tens,
In a small stock tank this was done,
'til they'd have enough fun,
Then they'd turn 'em loose again.

North of Wheeler this all happened,
fingers they were never tappin'.
They always found things to do.

The boys played cars and trucks,
the girls had rabbits and ducks,
And they were a happy bunch I tell you true.

Of course their was always cattle to check,
girls and horses right on deck,
Then they'd go to 'Yucca Town' and jump 'em.
Once when Lex was along on Dusty,
Cockleburr took a spill real crusty,
Lesa was one lucky little girl not to get jimed up!

That's about enough of their antics,
some times their parents were frantic,
But we all came out alive.
To the South Magley Farm in '73 we moved,
then everybody got in the grove,
Of *THAT* busy ~ bustling life!

South Place Farm

In the year of nineteen seventy three,
We moved to the south one, of Magley Farms Incorporated.
The price of wheat and cattle was good.
There was stock to tend and the irrigation was gated.

Dad moved into town so the little house was ours,
Seven rooms were way better than four.
To have a bathroom and shower was great,
With an upstairs and downstairs what's more.

Junior was the farmer and Ruben the stockman,
Helping each other out when needed.
Dad would help in heavy work times,
That's how the farm proceeded.

Ten people, two houses two barns and a shop,
Hay sheds, chicken house, a grain elevator.
Two Magley boys and two Landenberger boys,
They'd get into mischief, sooner than later.

Frying chickens were raised and a good big garden,
Along with our beef and pork.
So we had plenty of food to go around,
The supplies were never short.

We had started going to Little Britches Rodeos,
Tough competitors the girls had become.
So each weekend we'd pack-up the camper,
Load the horses, and follow the sun.

It was such fun to see the same people,
Each weekend, as we'd follow the shows.
We'd pull into a place, get their numbers,
Unload the horses and go with the flow.

And even though the competition,
Was tough between the rodeo kids.
They'd cheer each other on-
To do the *BEST* in whatever they did.

The girls gathered lots of awards,
In the course of our traveling years.
But the memories we have as a family,
Are the things we hold most dear.

Johnny's Fiddle

The violin hanging in sister-in-law, Alice's home,
It doesn't make a sound,
But let me tell you it was different,
When Dad Landenberger was around.

He really loved his fiddle,
It was his hearts delight,
To play a lively tune,
And make the spirits bright.
There was "Golden Slippers," "Red Wing,"
And "Cotton Eyed Joe."
It would get the people in the mood,
To do the "Doe-See-Doe."

"Over the Waves" and "Brown Eyes."
And the beautiful "Tennessee Waltz,"
Men would go get their partners,
And *dance* and have a *ball.*

And now it hangs there silent,
In a beautifully lighted case,
But if you search your memory,
Shining through is the *smile* on Johnny's face.

Tables

There are tables that say "I love you,
tables that pay the bills,
Holiday tables with lots of joy,
where we eat until we are filled.

There are ornate little tables,
that hold our mothers treasures,
Or a table out in the yard, where we sit,
if we have some leisure.

A table full of rows, of quart jars, of green beans,
Or other garden things, freshly canned, can be seen.
Happy Birthday tables with candles aglow,
How a two year olds face, with delight does show.

A supper table where the family gathers each night,
They talk of everyday things, both sad and bright.
Then of course at church, there is the Lords table,
Where we pour out our heart's contents, if we are able.

To allow him to forgive us for our human ways,
That sometimes tend to lead us astray.
When our sins are forgiven we feel uplifted,
And know for sure, that we are gifted.

With Love everlasting from above.
We thank *Him* at *all* tables for "Our Fathers Love."

Country Sights and Sounds

The sound of a cow in the distance,
the shine of a palomino's coat,
These are the pleasures of a morning walk,
along this serene country road.

The turkeys move slowly along as they feed,
some young ones frolic and play.
A bunny scurries across the road,
the deer won't be seen today.

And look at that water in Keller pond,
it looks just like a mirror !
And me and my Sheltie are walkin' along,
she couldn't be any dearer.

We both enjoy this feeling in the country,
there's just none other like it.
The air is fresh, the sun is up,
no *richer* could we strike it

Grandview Farm House

I'm a house on the hill, with a truly grand view!
For so many years I waited for you.
From my beginnings, I was tall and beautiful,
Your ancestors were strong and *OH*,So-dutiful.

I stand on this hill and can be seen for *miles*,
I know you've *heard* of my joys and trials.
For such a long time, I stood here alone,
Families came and went in life's everyday drone.

My frame was strong but my interior was ailing,
Then you came to me and *spirits* were sailing.
Your story in the paper captured the hearts of many,
Especially historians in and around Sainty.

To purchase me and go to work,
With loving care you gained back the look.
Of the way I was when the farm was busy.
With many an animal, machine, fowl, and tin lizzy.

There was plowing and sowing; cultivating and harvesting.
Plucking, cooking, baking, mending and sewing.
The range of emotions this house held within,
Have been told many times, as ink *flowed* from the pen.

But-Oh happy day, I've got *people* again,
That love my history and you've really been.
The best thing that ever could happen to me!
Thank goodness the bulldozer I didn't see.

The Wooden Nickel Gang

There's a guy that works for Silver Crest Farms,
He's got a quick-draw smile and means no harm.
Around the ten o'clock hour 'most every night,
Some of us have coffee, but Steve has a bite.

Or two or three or four or five,
'Cause he's been a workin', man alive.
He chases the black girls, cows that is,
And hauls the grain and all that bizz.

Don't take any wooden nickels-
If you do, 'with Steve' you're in a pickle.
Then there's Larry, the horse trader and rider too.
Always on the road, he's got lots to do.

When he's not doin' that he's campin' or fishin',
Or sittin' at the K-Store and really a dishin'
Out this or that to one and all,
Look out you may the next one in for a fall.

Then there's Jay, from old New Yoke,
He has trouble understandin' us Kansas folk.
Not only our language but our ways of doin' things,
About some of them, a smile it brings.

He plays and instrument in the town band,
And on certain things, he'll take a stand.
Next comes Diane, she's long, tall and brunette,
She cares about all of us, you can bet.

She hales from Montana, the Big Sky State,
She's got a big black dog, and he does rate.
She bought a house in town, cause she's stayin' a while,
She researches deeds for people that bring on smiles.

Then there's Dustin, he's quite a guy,
Seems he'll try about anything under the sky.
He's worked at feedlots, follows cattle on the move
Drives his grandpa's old trucks, or anything that'll grouve.

We rib him a lot, and he takes it good,
He rolls with the punches, the way ya should.
Jen comes a rollin' in about ten fifteen,
In her mean black pick-up, a lookin' real keen.

Sweet Pea, we call her from time to time,
Dark eyes sparkle with mischief
And her long hair looks fine.
She rides her horses, Moonshine and Bandy,
For many a mile, she has 'em in shape just dandy.

Not every night, but now and then,
The Krien guys come a saunterin' in.
They tell us of their horses, training young ones and such.
They take good care of them, they like 'em so much.

They'll razz one of us it they think we need it,
And we'll razz 'em back just to feed it.
Then there's yours truly, a cowgirl poet,
She shares now and then, so they all know it.

She's been down the roads, rows of crops and trails,
About family, land and horses, she's rhymed *lots of tales.*
But take 'This Bunch' it's one of a kind !
And to her way of thinking',
It's 'bout as good as you'll find.

Happy Hog Talk

There were two young hogs named Bacon and Ham,
So you know exactly the plans for them.
They were happy in their world, eating grain and greens,
Never showing any signs of making a scene.

They grew and were normal as pigs can be,
Eating about anything they could see.
Then one long day, when the humans were gone,
They broke into the tack shed, and that was *so-wrong.*

Said Bacon to Ham, "We're pigs, it's our job,
To get into what we can, to loot and to rob.
The door on this shed, it feels negotiable,
Let's work on it, 'til we can get sociable."

In there were sacks of corn to be broken,
So *happy hog talk,* between them were spoken.
"Grunt, bump, grunt, bump, *it's going to go,*
Smell that grain in there, *LET'S MAKE IT SHOW!*

These bags break easy by hoof or by teeth,
Chomp, chomp, yum, yum, it's as good as can be !
Better tastin' corn cannot be found,
It's gotta be the best, that's ever been around.

I'm getting' full, I'm bustin' out in back,
But let's keep on goin, we're really on track.
Hey-look at that strap, hangin' off of that saddle,
PULL IT DOWN AND THOSE BITS-MAKE 'EM RATTLE.

Just tearin' 'round in here feels so right!
Oh pal-*I'm sooo-full, my belly is tight.*
That corn tasted so-good, *it was just the best.*
Let's just lay down, and get some rest."

They had eaten their fill and messed where they pleased,
Those poppin' full porkers, just laid down with ease.
When the humans got home and found the squatters,
(The unconcerned vandals turned their heads around real slow)
Lookin' like they were sayin' " YA-GOT- ANY-WATER?"

Lee Connett-Calf Roper

Lee Connet was a cowboy of a certain kind,
'Bout as good 'a roper as you'll ever find.
He rode good horses with *blood to run,*
And practiced and practiced, 'til day was done.

He trained his horses with lots of hope,
To follow a calf and to work a rope.
When *his loop was thrown and the slack was taken,*
You'd know for sure that he was makin',

Tracks to get to the calf, in *a fluid motion,*
His horse would work with full devotion.
He could *"wrap 'em up" just 1,2,3,*
So very fast-you could hardly see,

What he was doin' in the fog of dust,
But when it cleared a little, you could trust,
That his hands would be a "Flyin' high in the air."
It sure was fun to *watch him, at the Fair.*

If something could be done, from the *back of a horse,*
He'd rather be there than on a tractor of course.
'Along' Bluff Creek, *he raised his brand of cattle,*
He loved the great outdoors, and being in the saddle.

Lee wore mighty fine boots and hats shaped to perfection.
Had an *easy going walk,* and a *laugh that was infectious.*
Whether husband, father, ropin' buddy or neighbor,
His personality was one, we'll always savor!

Dora Hand

by Josephine McIntire
From her 1943 poetry book 'Boot Hill'

Walk softly above us, my friends gather 'round,
But think not ye tread on unhallowed ground.
They branded us flotsam who lie in the sod,
Wrapped close in the infinite love of our God.

Perhaps by your standards, our virtues were few,
But no soul was course in the creed that we knew.

I came to Dodge City a singer alone,
With faith and with honor, unstained as your own.
I worked where I found it, and sang where I could.
In dance halls, saloons, but I looked for the good.
And deep in the hearts of these men of the plains,
Found good will and kindness, like hidden gold veins.
I have known outlaws, who at the day's end,
Were crying inside for the voice of a friend.
While mixing in liquor brawls, reckless and wild,
To hide from the world the warm heart of a child.

Perhaps by your standards, our virtues were few,
But no soul was course, in the creed that we knew.

I died in Dodge City a stranger alone,
With faith and with honor, unstained as your own.
I took for the summer, old Jim Kelly's house,
When a half breed named Kennedy on a carouse,
Supposing that Kelly was asleep in his bed,
Shot in through the window, but shot me instead.

He rode a fast horse, and galloped away,
But someone had seen him and so the next day,
Bat Masterson trailed him up Mulberry Branch,
And rounded him up at Spring Willow Ranch.

Perhaps by your standards, our virtues were few,
But no soul was course, in the creed that we knew.

Lee Brooks

By Josephine McIntire
From her book ~ Boot Hill @ 1943

I hit old Dodge in 69, up from the Western Trail,
Six thousand beef steers, fat and fine,
I helped to push along the line,
To find a northern sale.

We started from the Laurel Leaf,
Down near the coast, where Texas beef,
Was bred in it's own brand.
Took a week, to drive this herd,
As straight as any homing bird, across it's own range land.

We drifted northward on and on,
To Indian Nations range.
Monotony and ease were gone,
We used our wits and used our brawn.
To grapple with the strange wild tribes
Of Indians hunting there
And rustlers trying everywhere to cause a big stampede.

For if the running herd was split,
They could cut out a part of it,
To satisfy their greed.

We came to Dodge one Sunday night,
To cross the Arkansaw,
The stream was swollen out of sight,
The cattle headed back in fright,
And some began to paw.

Our foreman said to "Get to town,
We'll cross this gol-damn stream or drown".
The foreman's word was law.
Jeff Winters on his swimming mare,
Was told to point the herd,

He stroked her where her back was bare,
She took the stream nor turned a hair,
And no one spoke a word.
We forced the frightened cattle in,
They swam like preachers fightin' sin,
And followed Winters lead.

My bunkie on is cutten' hoss,
Was more than half the way across,
We heard a yell from "Spead."
The scream came from the right hand flank,
I took downstream just as he sank,
I tried to save my friend.

When he again came into view,
I saw him churned and beat into,
A half unconscious wreck.
I left my horse, and reached the spot,
And struggling there, at last he got,
His arms around my neck.

His form was stiff with fear and dread,
That stream raced like a mill,
He rode me like a lump of lead,
He rode we till we both were dead,
To waters deep and still.
Our souls crossed over Jordan's tide,
Landed on the other side,
Two buddies on a hill.

Throw 'em on The Trail-Original Song

The melody of this song came after reading the Kraisingers great book on the subject of this trail, and from then imagining what it must have been like on the long and lonely trail day after, day after day, in sunshine, wind, heat or rain. The lyrics of course tell the story of the route , the methods, and the path of the "Great Western Cattle Trail."

Head 'em up and move 'em out,
And throw 'em on the Trail,
This how it was on the Great Western Trail.
Millions of cattle, up this long trail trod,
Cutting a path in the early day sod.
While lotsa Texas guys, were fightin' in the Civil War,
The wild longhorns, their numbers did soar.
So they'd catch 'em and tame 'em;
And break 'em to the trail,
Point 'em to The Star, and find a northern sale.

Chorus,
Hi ya Hi ya Hup-Hup, Hi ya, Hi ya,-Hey!
Hi ya Hi ya Hup-Hup, Hi ya Hi ya-Hey!

They'd gather them in Texas, down by the coast,
So people back east could have beef to roast.
From old Dodge City on the western plains,
They'd load up the cattle on train after train.
When the herds *piled up*, they'd head 'em on north,
String 'em out, for all they were worth.
When the deadlines moved west of Ellis and Hays
They'd head 'em on north, for *days and days*.

Chorus

The ladder of rivers, led them on the long trail,
It wasn't for ones who were weak or frail.
The main trail went toward old North Platte,
Through the plains prairie, that was arid and flat.
In Northwest Kansas, by the town of Wano,
Republican crossed, on up north they would go.
Ogallala, Laramie, and Montana,
Then on up north to Canada.

Chorus

The Western Trail, was a *very long* trail,
It was the *greatest* of the cattle trails.
Millions of cattle-up this long trail trod,
Cutting a path in the early day sod.
Head 'em up and move 'em out, and throw 'em on the trail,
This is how it was on the Great-Western-Trail.